Costs and Financing of Higher Education in Francophone Africa

Costs and Financing of Higher Education in Francophone Africa

MATHIEU BROSSARD AND BOREL FOKO

PÔLE DE DAKAR
(UNESCO-BREDA)

WORLD BANK
Washington, D.C.

Acknowledgments

A preliminary version of this World Bank study was prepared for and presented at the "Higher Education for Africa's Development: Better Understanding the Keys to Success" conference held in Ouagadougou, Burkina Faso, on June 13–15, 2006. The findings, interpretations, and conclusions are the product of its authors and do not reflect in any way the views of UNESCO, or the World Bank, its affiliate institutions, its Board of Executive Directors, or the countries they represent.

The authors thank William Experton, who conceived and managed the project, for his thoughtful guidance and contributions; World Bank education experts Sajitha Bashir, Michael Drabble, Richard Hopper, Kurt Larsen, and Jamil Salmi for their many comments and suggestions; and Chloë Fèvre for her active support in moving the project forward.

We also express our gratitude to Pierre-Antoine Gioan (EduFrance) for his structuring comments and key inputs on the higher education planning strategy, as well as to Alain Mingat, Patrick Nkengne Nkengne, Claudine Bourrel, David Marchand, and Bonaventure Mvé-Ondo for their feedback and encouragement.

Finally, the authors are indebted to UNESCO's Breda Pôle de Dakar education sector analysis team, in particular Paul Coustère, Jean-Pierre Jarousse, Nicolas Reuge, Kokou Amelewonou, and Laure Pasquier for their valuable observations, and to Elsa Duret for her expert help with the reference material.

Contents

Foreword

Many people are aware of the looming funding crisis in higher education in Francophone Africa. Few, however, understand the seriousness of this situation. This study's data and analysis clarify the multiple dimensions and gravity of the crisis. This study follows up on and expands discussions that took place during the "Higher Education for Francophone Africa's Development" conference, which was held on June 13–15, 2006, in Ouagadougou, Burkina Faso. The conference was held at the initiative of the World Bank in collaboration with the government of Burkina Faso, the French Ministry of Foreign Affairs, and the *Agence Universitaire de la Francophonie*.

The study uses groundbreaking data collected in the Francophone countries of Sub-Saharan Africa by the United Nations Educational, Scientific, and Cultural Organization (UNESCO)-Africa's Dakar Hub analytical team and the World Bank during missions undertaken for Education Country Status Reports (*Rapports d'Etat des Systèmes d'Education Nationaux*, RESEN). As a result, for the first time, comparative data on costs and financing of higher education in a large number of countries are available to highlight the specific problems common to countries of this region and to identify the measures taken by some countries to address these problems. Because addressing the financing of higher education raises issues of equity in the use of public resources, management of student flows, and families' financial effort for their children's education, the analysis takes a sectorwide perspective.

The projected development of higher education through the year 2015 shows a major expansion of tertiary education demand. This demand will impose on those countries the need to design ambitious policies to avoid a decline in the quality of higher education and to guarantee employment for their young people.

This study represents a point of departure for more specific country studies. This departure will encourage proposals with viable solutions that can be adapted to specific situations. The study will facilitate a dialogue among the various stakeholders without which it would be impossible to make the necessary policy decisions. In this regard, the study is of interest to Ministries of Education and Finance, as well as to academia. Any solution will necessarily require everyone's effort and the relinquishment of certain special interests.

This study is also useful for countries and international financial institutions that are in a position to offer support in the development of higher education. These countries and institutions will be able to provide support only if the countries concerned have the political will to address the problem of financing. Indeed, it is difficult to mobilize external funds unless countries demonstrate that they can ensure the sustainable financing of higher education's operating costs.

Because the actors responsible for developing higher education often sidestep the difficult financing issues in their proposals, this study identifies the constraints in providing students with a quality higher education and highlights the efforts that must be deployed to achieve it.

Yaw Ansu
Human Development Sector Director Africa Region
The World Bank

Overview

Francophone African countries currently have a low enrollment rate in higher education of 3 percent, on average, in comparison with an 8 percent enrollment rate in countries of comparable levels of development. Despite this low enrollment, Francophone African countries face an immense challenge in terms of addressing these education needs. The increased social demand associated with the progress made in universal primary enrollment and the increase in secondary enrollment could cause the student population to grow from 800,000 in 2004 to approximately 2 million in 2015. This increase exacerbates the financial problems of higher education institutions and might cause the quality of training to decline. The problem of providing training that is relevant to labor market requirements has intensified. The difficulties faced by graduates of tertiary institutions in respect to entry into the modern labor market, which often provides less than 10 percent of the jobs, demonstrates the need for plans to increase the accommodation capacity of systems and for programs to better respond to countries' development needs.

This expansion of higher education is occurring within a context of extremely limited resources. Indeed, economic growth is still low and uneven in Francophone Africa, although the macroeconomic environment has improved in some countries since the mid-1990s. Moreover, public revenues are relatively low, representing less than 16 percent of gross domestic product (GDP) on average, in comparison with 22 percent in low-income Anglophone African countries. In this context, the education sector mobilized only 18 percent of public resources in 2003, whereas in Anglophone countries, the allocation for education on average accounted for 21 percent of national budgets. In addition, because of the more difficult macroeconomic and fiscal context, and a lower budget priority, the volume of public resources allocated to current expenditures in the education sector as a percentage of GDP is significantly lower in Francophone Africa (2.7 percent in 2003) than in Anglophone Africa (4.5 percent).

Finally, the share of public education expenditures allocated to higher education averages 21 percent, whereas this portion is only 17 percent in non-African countries of comparable levels of development. This priority, already relatively high, could hardly be increased while these countries are still far from attaining universal primary enrollment.

To better understand the challenges and opportunities facing higher education systems in Francophone Africa, this study takes stock of their situation, highlights the similarities and differences in strategies among countries, and indicates the potential for greater flexibility to improve financing as well as for internal and external efficiency of higher education systems. It then uses possible scenarios of future systems to highlight realistic and sustainable hypotheses for countries. Finally, it proposes policy tools that would enable policy makers and heads of higher education institutions to improve the quality and performance of systems while planning their development.

The methodology used is that of comparative analysis based on data collected for the Education Country Status Reports (*Rapports d'Etat des Systèmes d'Education Nationaux*, RESEN). These national studies were conducted by teams including managerial and technical personnel from the Ministries of Education and backed by the World Bank and other partners. They provide information on the development context of the education sector as a whole (macroeconomic, demographic, job market) and consolidate recent operational data to the extent possible (school statistics, financial data, management issues, and so on) and data on system performance (number of graduates, number of publications, number of research programs brought to fruition, and so on). In addition to the comparative analysis, simulation models were used to assess various scenarios for the development of higher education systems in Francophone Africa.

This study shows that public expenditure per student is quite high in most of the countries studied (on average 50 percent higher than in countries of comparable levels of economic development). The costliness of higher public education in Francophone Africa is due to several factors, the most important of which include: (i) the high volume of social (student assistance services) expenditure, which mobilizes 45 percent (on average) of current budgets for education in comparison with approximately 20 percent in other regions of the world; and (ii) the significant fixed costs attributable to the predominance of administrative personnel in institutions (60 percent of personnel on average). These costs leave few resources for academic activities and research, which are the guarantors of quality. Nevertheless, cross-country variations in the amount and composition of public expenditure per student show that a range of policies is available and gains are achievable in terms of efficiency and balance between academic and social expenditure.

Moreover, the analyses conducted indicate that, if the current rate of expansion continues and if the expenditure patterns and methods of providing student assistance services remain unchanged, the development of higher education in Francophone Africa will not be financially sustainable. For a sample containing 18 of the 21 Francophone African countries for which data are available, the financing gap for current expenditure on public higher education over the 2004–15 period would be about US$3.3 billion (in 2004 U.S. dollars).

In light of this, the study explores several strategic tools that would make it possible to improve the quality and performance of higher education systems while planning their development. The regulation of student flows, reduction of unit costs, cost-sharing, private sector development, and promotion of income-generating activities are just some of the possible areas that could guide the new higher education policies in Francophone Africa.

Budgetary and sociopolitical reasons, as well as the limited absorptive capacity of the labor market, make it imperative to regulate and manage student flows. Because of the resulting deterioration in education conditions and the lack of job prospects, allowing student flows to go unregulated would likely increase student dissatisfaction and could result in serious political crises. To plan for these situations and better handle the development of their higher education systems, many countries regulate admission to secondary education while concurrently developing vocational training and apprenticeship programs. Other countries (for example, Niger and Togo) have established a strict selection process for admission to higher education or for lengthy university training streams (for example, Madagascar). In Tunisia, the percentage of those awarded a baccalaureate is determined based on the places available at universities, and students who pass the baccalaureate exam are steered toward courses based on their test results. A similar system is currently being implemented at the University of Lomé in Togo.

Regarding the reduction of unit costs, this reduction should be organized in such a way that the portion of high-value expenditures is maintained. To do this, better targeting of social expenditure, reduction of the time needed to obtain educational qualifications, cost-sharing, private sector promotion, and better organization of distance learning are required.

Although social expenditure represents a little more than 45 percent[1] of current higher education budgets in Francophone Africa, there are significant disparities—as much as 1:4—among countries. It therefore appears that there is some scope for reducing expenditures in cases in which they are particularly high. To achieve this, greater selectivity in terms of student aid may be envisaged by introducing such criteria as academic excellence for scholarships. Chad, in particular, is considering the introduction of such criteria in its subsector strategy for higher education development. With regard to nonfinancial assistance, private sector incentive policies can lead to a dramatic decrease in social expenditure in such areas as housing (Burkina Faso) or food service and transport (as in the case of Côte d'Ivoire) (Gioan and Racamier 2005; Gioan 2006).

Improving internal efficiency and reducing "time-to-degree" can be powerful cost-reduction catalysts. These efforts can be facilitated by regulating student flows, monitoring reenrollment or multiple changes in course of study electronically, and enforcing a more selective scholarship policy. (The absence of such a policy encourages students to remain in the system, particularly if they are having trouble finding jobs.) Steering a larger proportion of students toward training streams of short duration can reduce the cost per graduate and improve the internal and external effectiveness of the systems.

Well-organized distance learning has great potential because of its relatively low marginal cost. It requires a sophisticated information technology, however, and countries, particularly low-income ones that plan to develop distance learning, must have a high student demand as well as access to the investment needed to train staff and adapt programs. Policy measures can be taken to build awareness of this learning method or even to encourage some students to opt for distance learning.

Private sector promotion and cost-sharing in higher education are other policy tools that promote sustainable development of the sector. In most French-speaking African countries, the percentage of students enrolled in private institutions of higher learning (19 percent) is smaller than at the secondary level (24 percent). This enrollment rate is lower than levels observed on average in non-African low-income countries, where 26 percent of students attend private schools. Thus, if governments set up a legal framework with incentives ranging from simplified administrative

---

[1] This percentage is likely to be underestimated: in many countries, student assistance services expenditures are "hidden" under other labels or are not included as line items in the higher education budget.

procedures for investment to the accreditation of programs and education credentials, including quality assessment, the potential exists for an expansion of private education in Francophone Africa. Governments can offer tax incentives for investment, open the scholarship system to students headed for private institutions, and even make facilities such as sites or buildings available. In Côte d'Ivoire, for example, subsidies have boosted the private sector, which moved from negligible enrollment figures in the 1990s to 30 percent of the student population today.

Higher education institutions should seek financing methods that supplement public financing. For this reason, they should be given greater autonomy to encourage them to diversify their resources by providing services and recovering a part of their costs from students. In the latter case, setting up student loans that must be repaid once students have entered the workforce is necessary to ensure that the measures are equitable and socially acceptable. At the same time, this will require an improvement in the quality of the training dispensed, which is the only way to ensure the international competitiveness of the countries in the region.

Improved governance and better decision-making tools are crucial to develop financially sustainable policies. Computerized information management systems can help higher education institutions reduce processing errors, reduce transaction costs, and contain overall costs. The efficiency of these systems has been demonstrated in several areas, including financial administration, human resource management (greater transparency in teacher performance and management of overtime), student files (monitoring repeat registration and changes in course of study), libraries, purchasing, university publications, and admission facilities. (At the University of Lomé in Togo, for example, computerized admissions management has allowed for improved use of available slots and instructional equipment.)

Finally, making higher education policies financially sustainable calls for timely decision making and a sound medium-term vision to support the options chosen. Simulation models can define financially sustainable policies with an overall sector perspective. Moreover, these models are communication tools that can be used to seek consensus between the different actors and partners in the system (for example, between technical staff and decision makers at the Ministry of Higher Education, and between the Ministry of Higher Education and other ministries, particularly finance, civil society, and the technical and financial partners). Only reforms subjected to broad-based consultation among the different actors can be expected to succeed.

Introduction

In the current context of a global economy based on information and knowledge, it is difficult for countries lacking an adequately qualified labor force to integrate the world market and be economically competitive. Numerous studies show that in an environment of rapidly evolving technologies and communication methods and in which trade and labor markets are becoming global, *education, and more specifically higher education, is a major vector of growth and economic competitiveness* (see TFHES 2000; World Bank 2002, 2003; De Ferranti et al. 2003; Bloom, Caning, and Chan 2005). Its contribution to growth and development cannot be overstated. Such growth will reduce poverty by generating the fundamental expertise needed in the sectors that spur development, including health, education, governance, private sector development, and the environment. It is in the countries' best interests to pursue efforts that raise the education level of their population.

The education situation in Francophone Africa is unique in the sense that most of these countries face two major challenges. The first challenge is quantitative. Although the expansion of higher education in Francophone Africa has been impressive (the gross enrollment rate in higher education nearly doubled between 1991 and 2004), the average coverage of higher education remains low throughout the region. An estimated 3 percent of individuals currently have access to higher education, whereas in other African countries with comparable levels of economic development, this proportion is 4 percent and is even as high as 8 percent in other low-income countries outside of Africa.[2] The second challenge is relevance. The education offered must better correspond to what national economies actually need. In Francophone Africa, the modern employ-

---

[2] Calculations are based on data from UNESCO's Institute for Statistics (UIS). The data are from 2004.

ment sector, which is the sector best suited for hiring graduates of higher education, is narrow and accounts for less than 10 percent (sometimes even less than 5 percent) of the total number of jobs. Thus, it is among such graduates that the highest unemployment rate (25 percent) and overqualification (30 percent) in terms of employment held can be found (Amelewonou and Brossard 2005).[3]

The expansion of higher education in Francophone Africa corresponds to a rising social demand. This demand should continue to grow during the coming decade because of the expansion in secondary education, which is a result of the increase in universal primary completion (UPC) rates, and because of a high level of private sector profitability—28 percent for one year of higher studies in Francophone Africa versus only 19 percent worldwide (Psacharopoulos and Patrinos 2002). The poor capacity of the labor market to absorb higher education graduates should spearhead debate on the quantitative expansion pace that would be beneficial from an economic point of view. Such facts call for appropriate policies formulated around the resources available, which are particularly limited in most of these countries. Because of the priority given to UPC rates and the fact that is difficult to change budgetary tradeoffs already favorable to the education sector as a whole, the share of public expenditure allocated to higher education will not increase in many countries. It will be necessary to diversify the financing sources, be it via private sector involvement, public institution generation of resources, or student cost-sharing.

These constraints suggest that plans to develop higher education in the majority of Francophone African countries must encompass policies that are financially sustainable, economically pertinent, and socially realistic. Much more so than in the primary and secondary levels of education, there is a strong variance in the way available resources are used and highly diverse methods for structuring the higher education services are offered. Formulating plans for sustainable development is a question of selecting the right policies from among a large number of options.

The primary objective of this study is to analyze the potential ways to expand higher education systems in Francophone Africa by using a well-documented inventory of the current situation and the projected sector-based trends throughout the subregion. For this, the following six questions will be addressed:

---

[3] These averages were calculated for 12 Francophone countries. The unemployment rate is higher than or equal to 30 percent in half of these countries. In 3 others, the rate of overqualification is greater than 35 percent.

- What is the amount of public resources made available for higher education in Francophone African countries, and what is the scope of increase over the next 10 years?
- How compatible are the composition and amount of public spending per student with the objective of quantitative expansion and the expectations of better quality and access?
- What is the share of private financing and household contributions that goes toward higher education?
- What are the potential constraints and scope for developing higher education in Francophone Africa for those countries striving to overcome the challenges mentioned above?
- Which tools are available to decision makers for building policies in favor of higher education that are financially sustainable and which respond to the populations' expectations?
- What are the principles and elements of a simulation model to help decision makers propose financially sustainable higher education policies?

This study includes two principal parts. The first part analyzes spending on higher education in Francophone Africa by using a doubly comparative approach: (i) over time (over the last 15 years), and (ii) between countries by comparing Francophone Africa with other developing regions and by analyzing the disparities within the Francophone African countries. Given the many shared characteristics of Francophone African countries (see box 1) the disparities seen in most of the indicators analyzed will reflect the differences between the implemented education policies.

The second part presents financial simulation models for elaborating (or improving) national plans to develop higher education in Francophone African countries.

This study does not, however, claim to provide complete answers to all the questions raised above. The answers to these questions call for nationally led technical efforts to achieve the following: (i) better analyze the situation of the higher education system (with better articulated and more current data), in particular by study program offered; (ii) better understand the situation of graduates and their prospects on the labor market; and (iii) better assess the different quantitative and qualitative options for development to be able to make propositions that are in line with the budgetary, economic, and social constraints, and to implement the propositions adopted.

BOX 1. COUNTRY CHOICE AND COMPARISONS WITH OTHER COUNTRIES

Why devote the study to Francophone African countries? These countries share many similarities. First of all, they are facing a challenge that is both quantitative and related to the economic relevance of the education offered in regards to the structural characteristics of national labor markets. In addition, they belong to a linguistic and cultural community inherited from colonialization. Out of the 21 countries included in this study, 13 belong to the Franc zone (whose currency is tied to the euro by a fixed exchange rate system), an institutional base that helps stabilize the macroeconomic framework. Furthermore, geographically, most countries in Francophone Africa are located in West Africa (nine) or Central Africa (eight). The higher education systems in the Francophone countries share characteristics that differentiate them from other countries in Africa. First, students are given free access to higher education upon passing the baccalaureate examination. Second, because registration fees are low, it is affordable to study in public higher education institutions. Third, universities and other higher education institutions have limited autonomy in relation to the ministry in charge of higher education. Such common characteristics of countries in Francophone Africa and the similarities between their higher education systems give good reason to conduct an analysis that studies these countries together.

Is it legitimate to compare Francophone countries with other developing countries? A rather clear structural relationship exists between the level of economic development and the fiscal context that governs the amount of revenue the state can use for operating collective services, the level of coverage, and the cost of higher education services. In effect, tax revenue is just as low as the country is poor and its fiscal base narrow; higher education is as developed as the country is rich; and poor countries must face relatively high costs to operate their education systems (for example, in the context of poor countries, university outlays such academic works and laboratory materials are often imported at international prices and are hence relatively costly given the level of national wealth).

From this perspective, it is possible to compare countries in Francophone Africa with other countries sharing a similar level of economic development. Because most countries in Francophone Africa fall in the "low-income countries" category, with a 2003 gross national income per head of less than US$756, this study specifically targeted other low-income African countries (the majority of which are in Anglophone Africa) and other low-income countries outside the African continent. The classification of countries according to income levels was based on the *World Development Indicators* (World Bank 2005). Countries referred to as "developing" had a 2003 gross national income per head of less than US$3,035.

Results expected of a comparison among countries in Francophone Africa, and between this set of countries and other groups of countries. The differences that will be highlighted in most of the analyzed indicators (fiscal pressure, public expenditure per student, private expenditure, the breakdown of public expenditure on education, and so on) are intended to reflect the differences in macroeconomic (fiscal policy) and education policies implemented between groups of countries (comparable levels of economic development) and between countries within Francophone Africa (similar in many ways and, with a few exceptions, also in terms of economic development).

Part One

Expenditures on Higher Education in Francophone Africa: Status and Trends

This part takes stock of Francophone African countries' expenditure on higher education. It is divided into three sections: (i) changes in public expenditure on higher education, (ii) dynamics and structure of public expenditure per student, and (iii) level of household contributions for higher education.

I. CHANGES IN PUBLIC EXPENDITURE ON HIGHER EDUCATION

Countries in Francophone Africa do not all face the same macroeconomic and budgetary limitations to operate their education systems. The changes in public resources allocated to higher education systems in these countries are examined in this context.

Expenditures analyzed are limited to those actually implemented in line with budgetary allotments.[4] Only current expenditures are taken into account: execution rates of investment expenditures are usually low and variable, and education sector investments are primarily financed by external aid (81 percent on average in the 10 countries in Francophone

---

[4] The differences between public expenditure and the budgetary allotments voted on by parliaments (see appendix table B3) are due to the quality of budgetary forecasts, the effectiveness of budget execution procedures, cash flow problems, or changes in priorities being implemented.

Africa for which data are available). Thus, current expenditures are somewhat outside the scope of this study, which seeks to assess national efforts in favor of education. In some countries, most investments in higher education are made via national resources,[5] but concrete data are lacking for most countries included in this study. In sum, current expenditures provide a good approximation of the overall public expenditure on education. Given the expected expansion of higher education and the resulting need for additional education structures, the scope of the investments needed must not be neglected.[6]

I.1. VARIED CONTEXTS: COUNTRIES IN FRANCOPHONE AFRICA ARE NOT FACING THE SAME MACROECONOMIC AND BUDGETARY CONSTRAINTS

The amount of public resources for higher education depends on four key factors: (i) national wealth, as measured by the gross domestic product (GDP); (ii) the government's capacity to use this wealth to operate collective services, as measured by the rate of public levy; (iii) the decisions made in favor of education relative to other public service areas financed by the state, as measured by the share of education in the public sector budget; and (iv) higher education priority relative to other education subsectors, as measured by the share of the total education budget allotted to higher education. When combined, these four parameters determine the amount of public funding available for the higher education subsector.

Over the recent years, the macroeconomic environment has improved in most Francophone countries (see figure I.1). Average growth rate has risen to 4 percent per year between 2000 and 2003, and this rate is closer to the average growth rate of Anglophone countries. This increase in economic activity is especially apparent in Rwanda and Chad.[7]

The **rate of public levy,** calculated here by the share of government resources in the GDP, is on average **lower in Francophone countries than in the Anglophone countries** (16 percent versus 22 percent, see figure I.2). The level of economic development in these countries was taken into account (a high level of development raises a country's tax levy potential). This rate, however, in Francophone countries is not particularly low when

---

[5] In the Côte d'Ivoire, for example, four new university structures were created in the 1990s (to broaden the education offerings) that were entirely financed by national resources (Gioan 2006).

[6] Unit costs of investments in this subsector are much higher than for primary and secondary education. In addition, although external aid constitutes a part of these investments, this aid is typically provided in the form of loans that increase public debt.

[7] In Chad, this increase has been catalyzed essentially by the oil boom.

Figure I.1: The Rhythm of Wealth Creation Varies from One Francophone Country to the Next

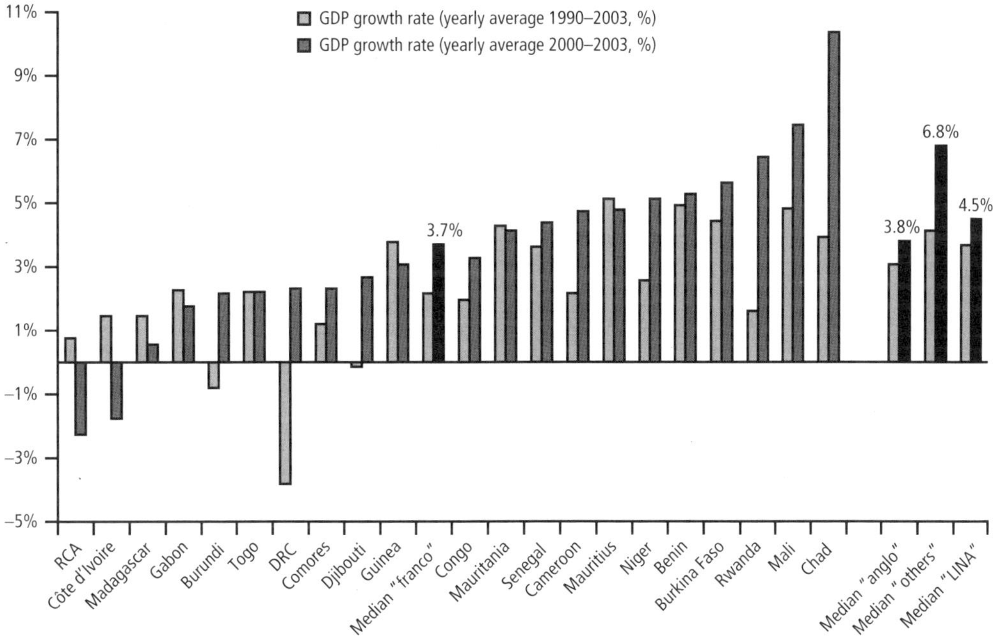

Sources: World Bank 2005; authors' calculations.
Note: GDP = gross domestic product; franco = Francophone African countries (average calculated only for low-income countries); anglo = low-income countries in Anglophone Africa (14 countries); other = other low-income countries in Africa (6 countries); LINA = low-income countries outside of Africa (mostly in Asia, 20 countries).

compared with other non-African low-income countries, which have a rate of public levy estimated at 15 percent of their GDP.

Rates of public levy in low-income Francophone Africa vary from 8 to 27 percent. Rates in Mauritania and the Republic of Congo are particularly high. In the Republic of Congo, the high rate is largely due to the key role played by the oil sector in the national economy, whereas in Mauritania, the tax levy potential will be increased by oil development activities, which currently are in the early phases. The high variability of rates of public levy among the countries, including among countries with comparable levels of economic development, suggests that potential exists to increase the tax base in countries where the latter is particularly narrow (notably in Burkina Faso, the Central African Republic, Rwanda, Chad, the Democratic Republic of Congo, Guinea, Madagascar, and Niger).

Although the relative position of Francophone countries compared with Anglophone countries as well as the change in the rates of public levy remained similar between 1990 and 2003 (the rate of public levy

Figure I.2: Low-Income Countries in Francophone Africa Are Not Facing the Same Public Financing Constraints

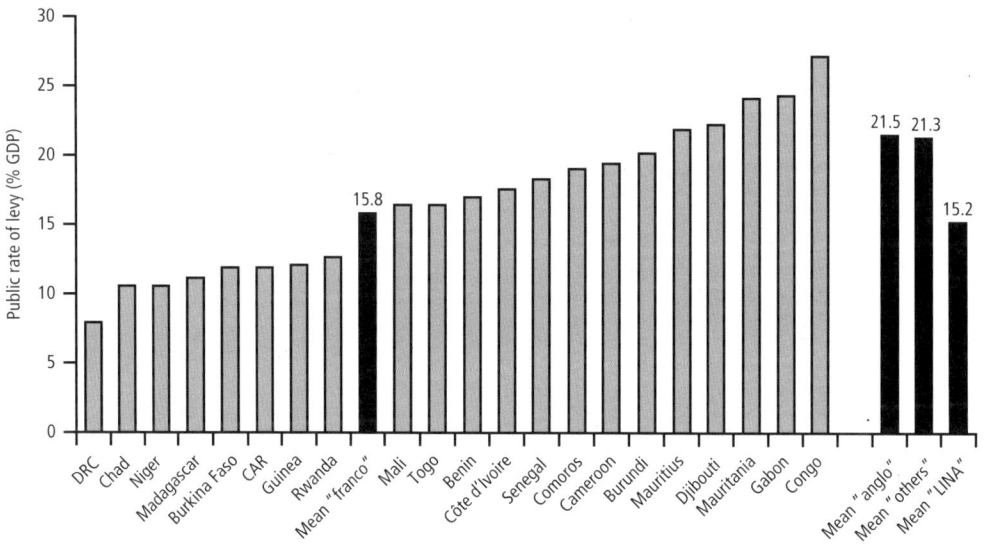

Sources: Appendix table B1; World Bank 2004, 2005; and authors' calculations.
Note: The term "rate of public levy" refers to all state revenues, tax or nontax, excluding grants. The data cover the period 2002–04. The average values were calculated only for low-income countries. GDP = gross domestic product; franco = Francophone African countries (average calculated only for low-income countries); anglo = low-income countries in Anglophone Africa (14 countries); other = other low-income countries in Africa (6 countries); LINA = low-income countries outside of Africa (mostly in Asia, 20 countries).

increased by only 0.9 points on average during this period), the return of economic growth that can be observed in most countries in the French franc zone following the currency adjustment in the mid-1990s (devaluation of the CFA franc) gives reason to expect better outlooks for these countries. The portion of the government's resources spent on education systems in low-income countries as a whole, and in those in Francophone Africa in particular, is presented in table I.1.

For the most recent year for which data are available, it appears that the share of current expenditure on education, as a percentage of public resources, is not significantly different among the large groups of countries studied. The average for low-income African countries, or 18 percent, is close to that of the world's other low-income countries. In Anglophone countries, this average is 21 percent, although it is only 18 percent in Francophone countries. This difference is mostly due to a significant decrease in the budgetary priority of education over the last 15 years or so in the Francophone countries. Indeed, in 1990, the education sector was mobilizing nearly 23 percent of public expenditure in these countries versus only 16 percent in the Anglophone countries (see figure I.3).

Table I.1: Changes in Public Expenditure on Education in Low-Income Countries, 1990–03

| Regions | Current public expenditure on education | | | |
| | As a percent of government resources | | As a percent of GDP | |
	Early 1990s[a]	Around 2003	Early 1990s[a]	Around 2003
Africa, including	19.3	18.2	3.1	3.3
Francophone countries	**22.9**	**17.6**	**3.3**	**2.7**
Anglophone countries	16.1	21.4	3.0	4.5
Other countries	12.9	11.7	2.4	2.0
Outside Africa	21.9	18.7	4.0	3.0
As a whole	**19.9**	**18.3**	**3.4**	**3.2**

Sources: Appendix table B1; authors' analyses or sector simulation models; UNESCO 1999; additional estimates are based on data from IBE 2001, UIS 2006, and World Bank 2004, 2005.
Note: GDP = gross domestic product.
a. designates a year between 1990 and 1992.

As a consequence of a macroeconomic and fiscal context that is problematic and gives less weight to education, **the amount of public resources spent on education, expressed as a percentage of the GDP, is, on average, lower in Africa's low-income Francophone countries** (2.7

Figure I.3: Changes in Public Current Expenditure on Education as a Percent of State Resources in Africa's Francophone Countries

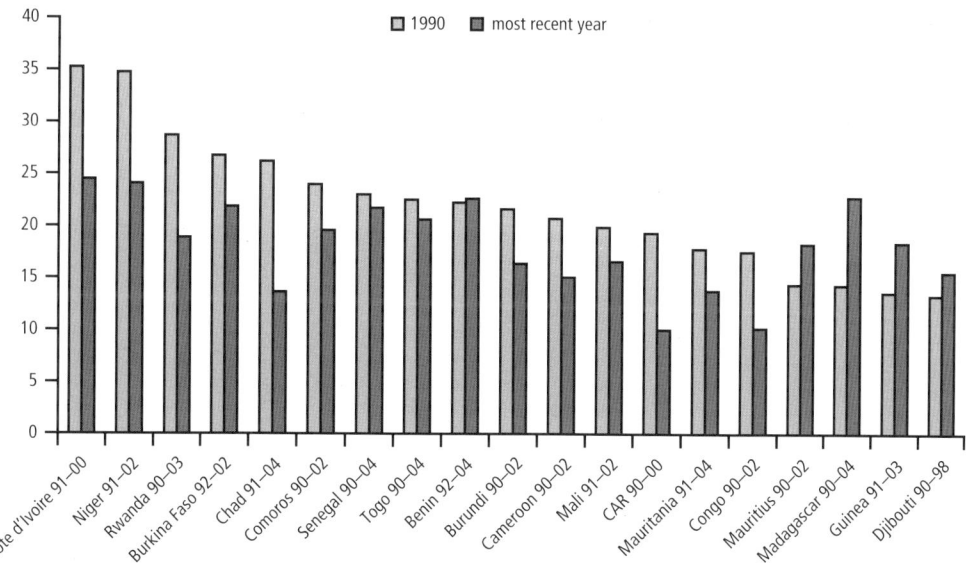

Sources: Appendix table B1; authors' analyses or sector simulation models; UNESCO 1999; additional estimates are based on data from IBE 2001; UIS; and World Bank 2004, 2005.
Note: The countries are listed in decreasing order according to the share of the public budget spent on education in 1990. This share was estimated to be 16 percent of government resources in Gabon in 2002 and 7 percent in the Democratic Republic of Congo in 2001.

percent in 2003) than the Anglophone countries (4.5 percent), as shown by the figures in table I.1.

The overall volume of public resources spent on education, as a percentage of the GDP, varies significantly among the countries included in this analysis (from 1 to 6 percent of the GDP), with no direct relationship with the countries' level of wealth. According to certain economists, this would confirm the fact that spending on education is a necessary and preliminary component of development (Bourdon 1999). Figure I.4 indicates, for example, that for countries with a per habitant income of between US$200 and US$300, current expenditure on education varies by a factor of one to three (from 1.4 percent of the GDP in the Democratic Republic of Congo and Chad to 5.2 percent of the GDP in Ghana).

Figure I.4 shows that African countries do not spend significantly more than other low-income countries to operate their education systems. This is demonstrated by the similarity between the figures indicated in table I.1 (respectively 3.3 and 3 percent of the GDP spent). The African average does not reflect the significant differences that exist between the Francophone and the Anglophone countries. Among the group of Francophone countries, the differences among nations are also significant: expenditures go from 1 percent of the GDP in the Central African Republic and the Democratic Republic of Congo to 4 percent or more in Côte d'Ivoire and Senegal. In Anglophone Africa, expenditures go from close to 2 percent in Eritrea and Zambia to more than 6 percent in Kenya, Lesotho, and Zimbabwe.

Figure I.5 contextualizes the differences among countries in terms of the overall volume of financial resources allocated to the education sector and suggests potential tools for increasing these resources on a national level.[8]

Among Francophone African countries, four groups of countries may be distinguished: (i) group 4, those with a doubly favorable context; (ii) group 3, those that place a lower priority on education; (iii) group 2, those that place a high priority on education; and (iv) group 1, those facing a dual disadvantage.

---

[8] Current expenditure on education as a percentage of the GDP depends on two key structural parameters: the rate of public levy and the priority given to education in budget allotments. Concerning comparisons across time of the levels of public expenditure on education (expressed as a percentage of the GDP), the budgetary priority is particularly high insofar as the rate of public levy is contingent on the macroeconomic development and varies little over the short term. For interregional comparisons, on the other hand, the rate of public levy is the key factor in that budgetary priority is nearly the same for all the groups, or at least those included in this study (see data in table I.1).

Figure I.4: Share of GDP's Public Current Expenditure on Education Based on the Level of Income per Habitant, 2003

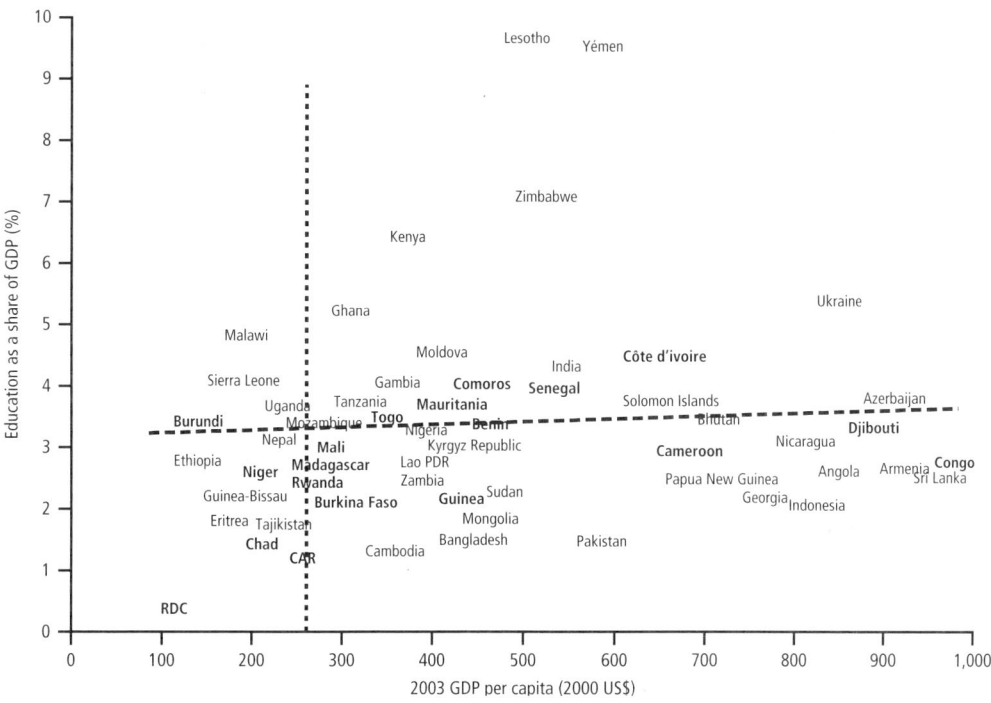

Sources: Appendix table B1; analyses or sector simulation models; UNESCO 1999; additional estimates are based on data from IBE 2001, UIS, and World Bank 2004, 2005.
Note: GDP = gross domestic product. Countries in Francophone Africa with GDP per capita below US$1,000 appear in bold.

The education systems of countries in **group 4** benefit from a **doubly favorable context;** both on the macroeconomic level thanks to a significant mobilization of resources for operating public services, and on the sector level thanks to the high priority of the education sector. Few countries are included in this group, and they allocate on average 38 percent of their GDP to the education sector (Benin, Côte d'Ivoire, Senegal, and Togo). The margins for increasing public resources for education appear narrow.

Countries in **group 3** enjoy a better fiscal context than most of the other Francophone countries. Nonetheless, because of the **lower priority placed on education,** they allocate roughly 3.5 percent of their GDP to operating their education systems, a percentage that is slightly higher than the average of all low-income countries in Africa. For most of these countries, the margins for increasing the amount of public resources spent on education hinges on an increase in the share of the government's budget allocated to education (particularly in Burundi, Cameroon, the Republic of Congo, and Mali).

Figure I.5: Macroeconomic Constraints and Education's Priority in National Budgets in Francophone Africa, 2002–03

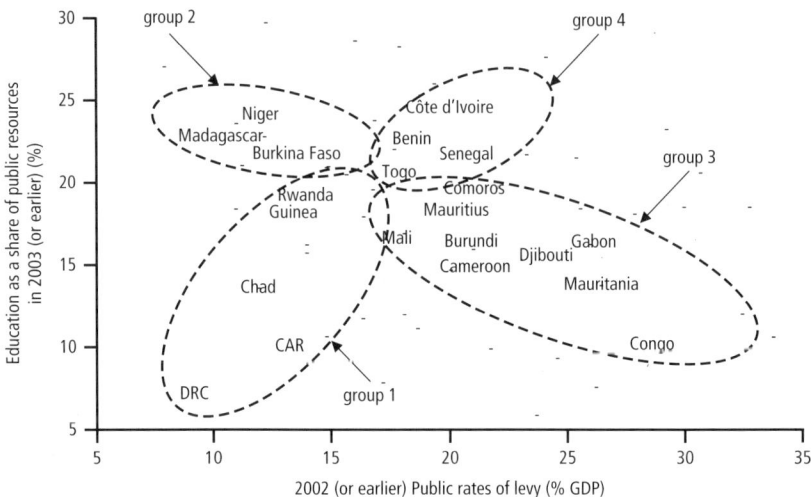

Source: Appendix table B1.
Note: GDP = gross domestic product; - designates a developing country not located in Francophone Africa.

Countries in **group 2** make up for their education systems' low rate of public levy by awarding a **high priority to education** in their budgets (notably Burkina Faso, Madagascar, and Niger). This political choice is essential in developing education in these countries, given that the rate of public levy will increase slowly over time as economies become more developed.

Countries in **group 1** are facing a **dual disadvantage:** their capacity to mobilize internal resources is weak and the priority they give education is below the average of Africa's low-income countries (or elsewhere in the world).[9] On average, these countries allocate only 1.5 percent of their GDP to operate their education systems, or less than half the average allocated by Anglophone countries and by those in group 4. In these countries, the margins for increasing the budgetary allotment for education presupposes budgetary decisions more favorable to the sector as well as efforts to increase the rate of public levy.[10]

---

[9] The situation in Chad is unique because current expenditure on education accounted for nearly 25 percent of the state's resources in 2003. Following the heavy increase in tax revenue caused by the oil boom (the rate of public levy went from 8 to 10.5 percent between 2002 and 2004), a decrease in current expenditure, down to 14 percent of government resources, was observed in 2004. However, investment expenditure has significantly increased.

[10] This rate is lower in Francophone Africa (16 percent) than in the Anglophone countries (22 percent), a difference that is not solely due to the level of revenue per head. Other fac-

1.2. EDUCATION COVERAGE DOES NOT ALWAYS REFLECT THE BUDGETARY EFFORT IN FAVOR OF HIGHER EDUCATION

The public effort in favor of higher education (that is, the share of the sector budget allocated to higher education) **is particularly high in Francophone Africa.** In recent years, around 2003, it amounted to 21 percent of the sector budget allowance, versus 19 percent in other developing countries, or 17 percent in other low-income countries. These figures can be found in table I.2. Francophone and Anglophone countries exhibit no significant differences.

This significant public effort for higher education does not translate into higher education coverage in Africa. As shown in table I.3, in 2004, the higher education coverage in low-income African countries amounted to half of that of non-African low-income countries (the enrollment rate was close to 4 percent in all low-income African countries versus 8 percent in the other countries). Thus, in terms of mobilized public resources, Francophone Africa's higher education systems perform poorly quantitatively.

Spending 1 percent of the GDP on higher education means that around 630 students per 100,000 inhabitants in Francophone Africa's low-income countries are covered, versus more than 2,000 students, or three times higher, in non-African countries. This low quantitative effectiveness of higher education systems in Francophone Africa results in higher public expenditure per student (costliness of higher education) than in non-African countries with comparable levels of economic development.

On average, developing countries allocate 20 percent of their public current expenditure on education to operate higher education systems (see table I.3). This proportion does not appear to be compatible with the Millennium Development Goals for UPC (in countries that are most behind in this area) nor with developing other levels of education (in countries that have a more evolved education pyramid with a fairly wide base).

As seen in figure I.6, some countries, though far from meeting the UPC goal, allocate more than 20 percent of their current expenditures on education to higher education.[11] This is the case in Benin, Burundi, the Central African Republic, Chad, Guinea, the Republic of Congo, Rwanda, and Senegal in Francophone Africa. Equatorial Guinea, Guinea-Bissau,

---

tors play a role and may be exogenous (such as pluviometry, terms of exchange, and oil development) or stem from economic policy choices (for example, the structure of the economies, and their level of openness and monetarization).

[11] A country is considered to be far from reaching this goal when the primary education completion rate is less than 75 percent, meaning that at least one out of every four children does not yet have access to the last grade of primary education (see UNESCO-Breda 2005).

Table I.2: Share of Public Current Expenditure on Education Allotted to Higher Education (percent)

Regions	Early 1990s[a]		Most recent year[b]	
	Low-income countries	Developing countries	Low-income countries	Developing countries
Africa, including	21.7	21.6	20.7	20.8
Francophone countries	**23.9**	**23.3**	**21.2**	**21.2**
Anglophone countries	20.5	20.6	18.2	17.9
Other countries	—	17.4	—	25.9
Outside Africa	13.5	16.4	16.5	18.7
Combined average	**19.1**	**18.7**	**19.7**	**19.7**

Sources: Appendix table B1; estimates are based on data from the IBE 2001, UNESCO 1999, and UIS.
Note: The criterion used to classify the countries was described in box 1; — signifies that there were not enough countries for which data were available.
a. 1990 to 1993.
b. 2000 to 2004.

Table I.3: Mobilized Public Resources and Higher Education Coverage (low-income countries, most recent year 2000–05)

	Africa			Countries outside Africa
	Francophone	Anglophone	Africa[c]	
Recurrent public expenditure on higher education				
As a percent of public current expenditure on education	**21.00**	18.00	21.00	17.00
As a percent of the GDP	**0.53**	0.83	0.63	0.41
Higher education coverage in 2004[a]				
Students per 100,000 inhabitants	**336.00**	514.00	441.00	936.00
Coverage for 1 percent of GDP allocated to higher education[b]	**634.00**	619.00	700.00	2,283.00
Enrollment rate (percent)	**2.80**	4.20	3.70	8.20
Coverage for 1 percent of GDP allocated to higher education[b]	**5.30**	5.10	5.90	20.00
Coverage of higher education in 1991[a]				
Students per 100,000 inhabitants	**179.00**	158.00	164.00	559.00
Enrollment rate (percent)	**1.60**	1.40	1.50	4.90

Sources: Calculations based on data from the UIS, the United Nations, and the World Bank; appendix tables B1 and B2.
Note: GDP = gross domestic product
a. Average estimates using relevant demographic weights.
b. Obtained by relating the number of students per 100,000 habitants (or enrollment rate) to public current expenditure on higher education expressed as a percent of the GDP.
c. All low-income African countries taken together.

Mozambique, and Sierra Leone were in this position in 2003. Cameroon, on the other hand, with its broader education pyramid, could increase its effort to finance postprimary levels, namely higher education, which received only 14 percent of current expenditure on education in 2003.

Figure I.6 shows how much public spending on higher education varies across countries, ranging from 5 to 40 percent of current expendi-

Figure I.6: In Some Countries, Public Spending for Higher Education Is at Odds with the Current Education Pyramid

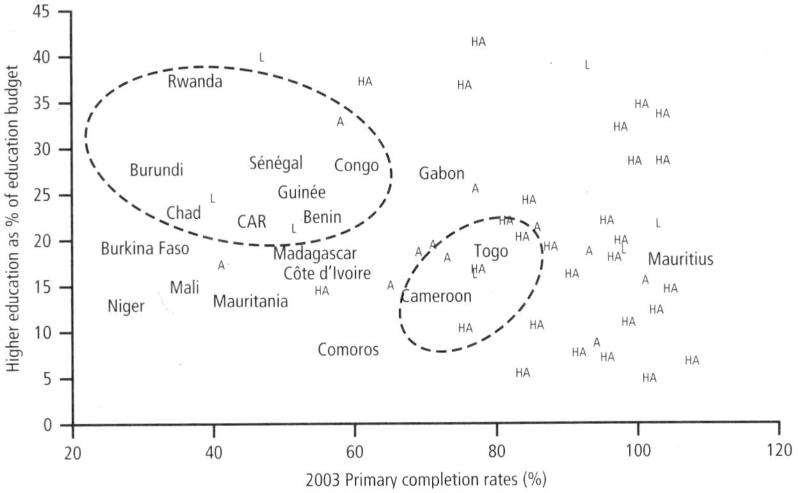

Sources: Appendix table B1; UNESCO-Breda 2005; and World Bank 2005.
Note: A = country from Anglophone Africa; L = other African country; HA = non-African developing country.

ture on education in all developing countries with available data. Countries in Francophone Africa have a similar distribution: from 8 percent in Comoros to 35 percent in Rwanda.

There does not appear to be any particular correlation over time in terms of public effort for higher education.[12] This may indicate that countries can in fact vary their intrasectoral allocation of resources to eventually achieve greater consistency with the shape of their education pyramid, as well as economic equity.[13] As suggested by figure I.6, this process should no doubt lead to reexamining public efforts in favor of higher education in the numerous countries of Francophone Africa, which are far from reaching the Millennium Development Goal for education. Consequently, public resources for higher education will be restricted in several Francophone African countries, except in those for which the macroeconomic situation improves and the budgetary decisions made are more favorable to the education sector.

---

[12] The temporal correlation between the public effort for higher education in 1990 and the effort observed in 2003 is only 14 percent in all developing countries and 12 percent for the countries of Francophone Africa.

[13] In certain countries, between 1990 and 2003 (or similar years), the share allotted to higher education in the recurrent education budget increased significantly (for example, from 15 to 35 percent in Rwanda, and from 11 to 23 percent in Chad), whereas in others it was reduced (for example, from 23 to 16 percent in Mauritania, 28 to 17 percent in Madagascar, and 30 to 19 percent in Togo).

II. DYNAMICS AND STRUCTURE OF PUBLIC EXPENDITURE PER STUDENT

Average public expenditure per student (unit expenditure) is an indicator of the public cost incurred for the education of one student over a one-year period (table I.4).[14] In this section, we first examine the average unit expenditures (without distinguishing among the various types of institutions). We then break down these expenditures by functional destination (separating salary expenditures from education and social expenditures) and by available education streams.

II.1. LEVEL AND CHANGE OVER TIME OF AVERAGE UNIT EXPENDITURF[15]

II.1.1. There are significant costs differences between Francophone African countries and countries with a comparable level of economic development

With an average public expenditure per student 2.8 times the average 2003 per capita GDP, **public higher education in Francophone African countries incurs four to five times more costs compared with the non-African countries that have similar levels of economic development.**[16] Within the African continent itself, however, there are no statistically significant costs differences between Francophone and Anglophone countries, underlining a relatively expensive public higher education in Africa.

II.1.2. Unit expenditure is particularly high in some countries

Although low-income Francophone African countries as a whole exhibit a level of economic development comparable to that of the low-income non-African countries considered in this study,[17] significant income differences do exist among the various countries. Per capita GDP ranges

---

[14] This refers only to *current* unit expenditure and excludes investment expenditures.

[15] Unit expenditure is expressed here as a percentage of per capita GDP, enabling comparisons among countries on the relative costliness of public higher education. It is appropriate as a measure because (i) the sustainability of national education policies depends on national wealth as reflected by per capita GDP and (ii) unit expenditure in percent of per capita GDP reliably compares countries against the relative costliness of their public higher education. Such comparison is preferably carried out among countries with similar levels of per capita GDP. In this respect, given two countries with a similar level of per capita GDP, the one whose university outlays (salaries, lab materials, university textbooks, and so on) are more costly (in relation to its domestic wealth) is *considered* to have a higher operating cost, all else being equal.

[16] The 10 low-GDP non-African countries referred to here are located in Eastern Europe and in Asia: Bangladesh, Cambodia, India, Kirghizstan, Lao People's Democratic Republic, Moldova, Mongolia, Myanmar, Nepal, and Tajikistan.

[17] This is the case only for low-income countries.

Table I.4: Public Expenditure per Student in Public Higher Education (percent of per capita GDP)

Regions	Beginning 1990s[a]		Most recent year[b]		
	Low-income countries	Developing countries	Low-income countries	(Number)	Developing countries
African countries	438	368	300	(28)	273
Francophone	**420**	**426**	**275**	**(18)**	**275**
Anglophone	541	403	308	(8)	261
Other countries	—	117	456[c]	(2)	275
Non-African countries	78	61	45	(10)	43
Overall	**323**	**208**	**233**	**(38)**	**194**

Sources: Appendix table B1; World Bank 2000, 2004.
Note: — = not available.
a. 1990 to 1993.
b. 2000 to 2004.
c. The average figures for Mozambique (791 in 2003) and Guinea-Bissau (121 in 2002) should be taken with caution.

from a factor of one to nine among low-income Francophone African countries, and from one to four among the non-African countries. Calculating *expected* average unit expenditure (while considering each country's level of development) therefore makes it possible to better assess the relative costliness of higher education in Francophone Africa. This cost is obtained by using a statistical relation of unit expenditure and per capita GDP.[18]

Table I.5 shows the results obtained for Francophone countries for which data are available. **As a whole, costs for higher education in all Francophone African countries are 50 percent higher than other countries with similar levels of economic development.** This global picture does not depict the significant disparities among these countries. A classification of the countries according to the relative costliness of their public higher education highlights the high cost of education (or at least, in recent times) in Burkina Faso, Burundi, Chad, Guinea Conakry, Niger, the

---

[18] Unit Expenditure (or Unit Cost) in any given country is largely dependent on its level of economic development. As mentioned in box 1, poor countries incur high relative costs for the provision of education services. It is therefore inappropriate to make gross unit cost comparisons between countries that are at different stages of development (for instance, between the Democratic Republic of Congo and Mauritius) because these comparisons do not reflect the fact that costs differences, to some extent, are a result of differences in wealth. Thus, costs incurred by country A should only be compared to the average unit cost of countries with a similar level of economic development as that country. In cases in which no countries have similar levels of economic development (in terms of per capita GDP) as country A, a statistical relation is used to relate the country's unit expenditure to its per capita GDP level. This relation, developed on the basis of all developing countries, simulates the average unit expenditure of other countries on the presumption that these countries have the same per capita GDP as country A.

Table I.5: Public Expenditure per Student and Relative Costliness of Higher Education in Francophone Africa (most recent years)[a]

	Per capita GDP (US$, 2000)	Year	Public expenditure per student Obtained (1)	Simulated (2)[b]	Costliness index (1)/(2)[c]
Rwanda	260	2003	750	197	3.81
Burkina Faso	253	2003	550	200	2.75
Niger	178	2003	565	247	2.28
Burundi	100	2004	719	350	2.05
Republic of Congo	943	2005	184	92	2.00
Senegal	485	2004	246	136	1.81
Chad	218	2004	386	219	1.76
Guinea Conakry	431	2004	231	146	1.58
Côte d'Ivoire	597	2001	137	120	1.14
Mali	258	2004	193	198	0.98
Benin	392	2004	149	154	0.96
Madagascar	233	2003	189	210	0.90
Comoros	365	2003	130	161	0.81
Central African Republic	229	2003	156	212	0.73
Cameroon	634	2003	84	116	0.72
Mauritania	372	2004	109	159	0.68
Togo	292	2003	112	184	0.61
Dem. Rep. of Congo	87	2003	57	382	0.15
Average	**378**	n.a.	**275**	**194**	**1.42**
Djibouti	848	2000	—	98	—
Gabon	3 865	2001	52	35	1.51
Mauritius	4 161	2003	49	33	1.47
Francophone Africa	**724**	n.a.	**(252)**	**(174)**	**1.45**

Sources: Appendix tables B1 and B2; authors' calculations.
Note: GDP = gross domestic product; n.a. = not applicable; — = not available.
a. The countries are classified in diminishing order of the relative costliness of their higher education.
b. The simulation data are based on an econometric estimate.
c. An index higher than 1 indicates that public higher education services incur more costs in the country compared with similar services provided in countries with the same level of economic development.

Republic of Congo, Rwanda, Senegal, and, to some extent, Côte d'Ivoire. The high variation in unit expenditure (ranging from a factor of one to five, comparing Côte d'Ivoire and Rwanda) points to differences in the policy decisions and indicates the possibility of improving on efficiency.

For some countries, circumstances surrounding higher education tend to account for, at least to some extent, the relative costliness of the services offered. In Rwanda, for instance, such costliness is partly due to the following: (i) the employment of foreign teachers, (ii) the relative spreading out of the training programs offered, and (iii) increased efforts to train teachers abroad to reconstitute the country's teaching personnel in the aftermath of the crisis endured by the country (genocide). Some countries in a post conflict situation are likely to face similar difficulties. Conversely, in some African countries, public education services are provided at lower (or similar) unit costs than those observed in countries with a comparable level of economic development. This is the case notably in Cameroon, Central African Republic, Comoros, the Democratic Republic of Congo, Madagascar, Mauritania, and Togo.

II.1.3. Costliness of education curtails the growth of education systems if important sources of financing are not available

Given current levels of unit expenditure, the growth of higher education systems in Francophone Africa supported almost exclusively by public funding faces serious limitations. Figure I.7 shows that coverage in the provision of higher education is insufficient in most of Francophone

Figure I.7: High Unit Expenditure Curtails Quantitative Growth of Higher Education

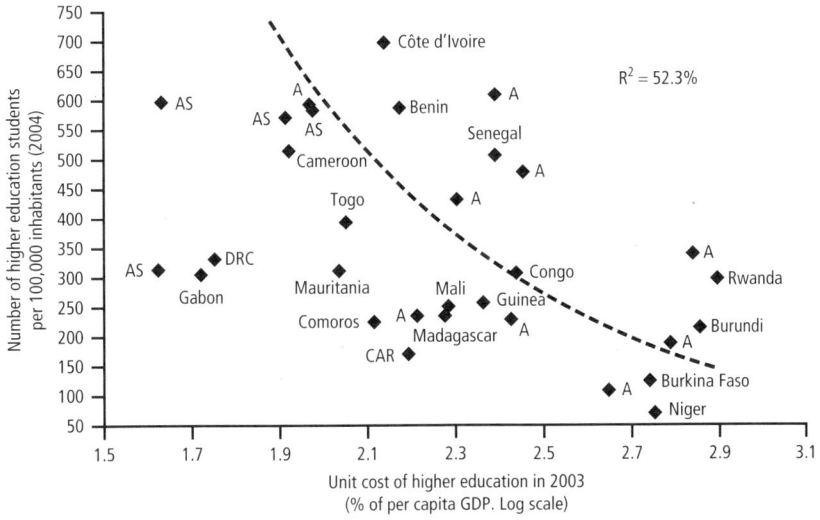

Sources: Appendix tables B1 and B2.
Note: The figure includes a sample of 41 developing countries, including 28 African countries. For more clarity, it is limited to countries with less than 750 students per 100,000 inhabitants.
AS = Asian developing countries; A = other African countries; GDP = gross domestic product.

Figure I.8: Unit Expenditure in Public Higher Education Fell in the Majority of Francophone African Countries between 1990 and 2003

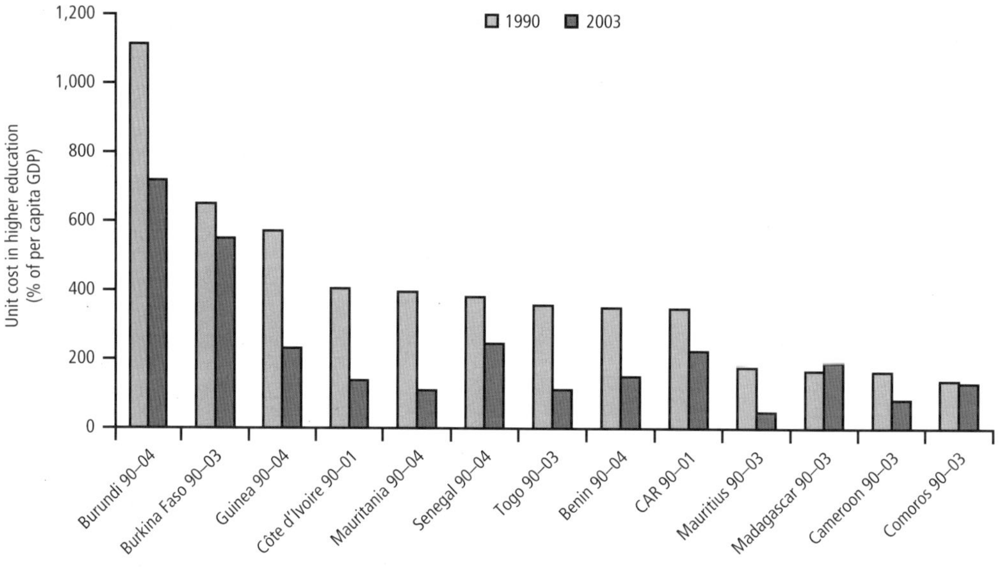

Source: Appendix table B1.
Note: GDP = gross domestic product.

Africa. Low-income non-African countries with lower unit expenditure have twice as much education coverage.[19]

II.1.4. Unit expenditure has been falling in Francophone Africa for the last 15 years

Figure I.8 shows that, between 1990 and 2003, unit expenditure as a percentage of the per capita GDP fell. Dropping by about 30 percent in all low-income countries, and even more so in Francophone African countries (from 420 to 275 percent of the per capita GDP, or a one-third drop). In Benin, Cameroon, Central African Republic, Côte d'Ivoire, Guinea Conakry, Mauritania, Mauritius, and Togo, unit expenditure fell by as much as half and even further (see figure I.8).

---

[19] Table I.3 compares coverage of 336 students per 100,000 inhabitants in 2004 in the low-income countries of Francophone Africa with 936 of the low-income non-African countries. There was no basis for assuming a close relationship between coverage and unit expenditure, however, because the calculation of the chosen coverage indicator (that is, the number of students per 100,000 inhabitants) is not solely based on public higher education institutions. If that had been the case, a systematic accounting relation would have been obtained. For any given budget, the higher the number of students enrolled, the lower the unit expenditure incurred.

The fall in unit expenditure, as a percentage of the per capita GDP, indicates **diminishing public expenditure per student** (in constant monetary units) with little increase in real per capita GDP (less than 2 percent) in the 1990–2003 period for all the low-income Francophone African countries. Some countries like Burundi, Comoros, Côte d'Ivoire, and Madagascar have even been experiencing negative growth.

How can such a fall in unit expenditure in Francophone African countries be accounted for? First and foremost, there is a *mechanical effect:* enrollments in higher education institutions increasing at a faster pace than higher education budgets mathematically result in lower unit expenditure. As a matter of fact, higher education coverage virtually doubled between 1990 and 2003[20] while resources earmarked for higher education as a percentage of the GNP fell globally within the same period. In Côte d'Ivoire, for instance, current public expenditures for higher education rose by only 85 percent between 1992 and 2000, whereas the number of students enrolled in higher education institutions went up by 300 percent (from 24,000 to 76,000 students).

The fall in unit expenditure may be accounted for by *better management*. In Côte d'Ivoire, still in the same period, the drop was most probably the result of rigorous budget management and better resource allocation, including the following:

- Rationalized management of higher schools of learning (auditing budgets and operations, followed by the implementation of rationalization plans)
- Reduction of social expenditures (freezing scholarships, transferring catering services into private hands, and ending free transport services)
- Encouraging private sector intervention

In higher education systems that are still at an embryonic stage (as were the higher education systems of Francophone Africa in the 1990s), reduction of unit expenditure reflects the initial occurrence of considerable fixed costs,[21] and thus economies of scale tend to accrue with the quantitative growth of the systems. Efforts to reduce the unit expenditure should avoid reducing pedagogic expenditures that are critical to improving the quality of education (or at least avoiding its deterioration). Even

---

[20] Compare with table I.3.
[21] Undeveloped higher education systems incur considerable fixed costs. For instance, minimum staff are hired to make such systems function, regardless of the number of students.

Table I.6: Change in Public Unit Expenditure and Relative Costliness of Public Higher Education in Francophone Africa, 2003

Change from 1990–2003	Relative costliness (most recent year)[a]		
	High	Low	Near average
Little variation		Comoros Madagascar	
Significant fall	Burkina Faso Burundi Côte d'Ivoire Guinea Conakry Senegal	Cameroon Mauritania Central African Republic Togo	Benin
No available information[b]	Rep. of Congo Niger Rwanda Chad	Dem. Rep. of Congo	Gabon Mali Mauritius
Conclusion: control the costliness of the services offered [c]	*—Reduce costs* *—Promote the development of the private sector*	*—Formulate favorable budget allocation policies* *—Explore the possibilities for sharing costs* *—Promote the development of the private sector*	*—Ensure favorable costs allocation for pedagogic outlays* *—Promote the development of the private sector*

Sources: Based on table I.5 and figure I.8.
Note:
a. Compared with countries having a similar level of economic development. The most recent year varies between 2000 and 2004.
b. Data for Djibouti are not available.
c. To be adapted to the national context. In Part 2 (section II.2.2), these conclusions will be better supported.

though unit expenditure fell between 1990 and 2003, it remains high in many Francophone African countries (table I.6 summarizes this information over the years and for the various countries). This falling tendency is expected to continue in the upcoming years which should improve the education systems' efficiency.[22]

---

[22] Although unit expenditure increases with level of education, in most low-income countries (see appendix table B4), unit expenditure for secondary education is much nearer to that in primary education (a ratio of 2.5:1 in low-income countries) than to higher education systems (a ratio of 1:8). Thus, one year of higher education studies (per student) financed by the state costs 19 times more than one year of primary school studies (per pupil). At the primary level, unit expenditure tends to be homogenous between countries, but it varies a lot at the other education levels. Such an important variation in unit expenditure per student in higher education (whereas it is much closer from one country to another at the primary level) is an indication of the fact that different policies are being pursued and that alternatives do exist to control higher education costs.

II.2. STRUCTURE OF UNIT EXPENDITURE IN FRANCOPHONE AFRICAN COUNTRIES

Box 2 breaks down public unit expenditure in terms of key education policy parameters: unit social expenditure (which depends on the average amount of assistance per beneficiary student and the proportion of beneficiary students), student-teacher ratio (number of students per teacher), institutions' unit operating expenditure, teaching staff salary, and share of administrative and technical staff in the institutions. This breakdown can be adjusted to reflect existing course programs and education streams and types of institutions.

II.2.1. The structure of public unit expenditure varies with each country

Three of the five major categories of public expenditures identified in box 2 (salary expenditures, current expenditures—including education expenditures—and social expenditures)[23] can be analyzed from the available data. Figure I.9 summarizes the available information. Because the unit costs do not include expenditures for studies abroad, scholarships and other assistance given to students abroad are not included. Scholarships and other assistance that are given for studies abroad will be analyzed separately, however, because these policy options can be used extensively to generate cost savings—that is, to reduce the recurrent operating expenses of the systems.

The make-up of current expenditures in higher education is extremely varied. Figure I.9 is a reasonable depiction and illustrates this variation although the structure of expenditures does not sufficiently reflect the scale of actual social expenditures for some countries. In fact, some social expenditures are "hidden" under other headings.[24]

For Francophone African countries in particular, social expenditures (for those students studying in their homelands) account on average for a little less than 40 percent of unit expenditure. Salary expenditures account for a little bit more. There are, however, significant variations from these averages in the allocations made from one country to another: for instance, salary expenditures account for only 24 percent of unit expenditure in Mali compared with 75 percent in the Republic of Congo. Inversely, current expenditures (at the level of both institutions and cen-

---

[23] These expenditures cover scholarships awarded to students or other subsidized services provided to students (for example, housing, meals, transportation, medical services, loans, and so on).

[24] For instance, in Côte d'Ivoire, SOTRA (an urban transport company) received a subvention of more than 2 billion FCFA each year as compensation for reduced cost of transport card fares for students. This amount was never entered in the budget of the Ministry of Higher Education.

BOX 2: BREAKDOWN OF PUBLIC UNIT EXPENDITURE IN HIGHER EDUCATION

Total current expenditure on education can be determined using the following formula:

Current expenditures = Teaching staff wage bill at the level of the institutions
+ Nonteaching staff wage bill at the level of the institutions
+ Operating expenditures at the level of the institutions
+ Social expenditures (scholarships and other university-level assistance)
+ Central administration expenditures (administrative staff salaries and management expenses)

To calculate public unit expenditure (or, more simply, the unit cost), expenditures by way of grants to private institutions as well as assistance given for studies abroad are subtracted from current expenditures and the result obtained is divided by the number of students in the public higher education institutions of the country.

Current public unit cost = Unit salary cost for teaching staff
+ Unit salary cost for nonteaching staff in institutions
+ Unit cost for institutions' operation
+ Unit cost for social expenditures
+ Unit cost for administrative expenditures

Teaching staff unit salary cost = Mean teaching staff wage bill/Number of students
= Mean teaching staff salary * Number of teachers/ Number of students
= Mean teaching staff salary/Number of students per teacher

Thus, for current unit cost,

Current public unit cost = Average teaching staff salary/number of students per teacher
+ Average non-teaching staff salary/number of students per nonteaching staff
+ Unit cost for institutions' operation
+ Unit cost for social expenditures
= Average teaching staff salary/number of students per teacher
+ Unit cost excluding teaching staff salary and social expenditures
+ Unit cost for social expenditures

This can be broken down further, as in the case of social expenditures (including scholarships):

Social expenditures = Average amount of assistance per beneficiary student *
Number of students * percent of beneficiaries. We get the
unit cost for social expenditures:

Unit cost for social expenditures = Average amount of assistance per beneficiary
student * percent of beneficiaries

Note: The breakdown follows the principle that if education current expenditures consist of various components, it is appropriate to calculate the various components of unit expenditure. The breakdown enables (depending on available information) the distinction of expenditures made at public higher education institutions from expenditures made in the financing of administration and management services (administrative and educational) activities both at the central level and at decentralized levels.

tral administration) account for only 10 percent of unit expenditure in the Republic of Congo compared with 25 percent in Mali.

II.2.2. Detailed analysis of unit expenditures

II.2.2.1. Social expenditures account for a significant proportion of higher education budgets

Overall, social expenditures (including those for local studies—scholarships and other university assistance—and scholarships for studies abroad) account on average for 45 percent of overall current expenditures in the 16 Francophone African countries for which data are available. The range of variation goes from 13 percent in Madagascar to 70 percent in Niger (a ratio of almost one to five). **Thus, social expenditures seem very high in Francophone African countries.** In Asia, these expenditures account for only 6 percent of public higher education current expenditures, 15 percent in countries of Eastern Europe and Central Asia, 17 percent in OECD countries, and 20 percent in countries of Northern Africa, the Middle East, and South America (World Bank 2002; OECD 2006). Furthermore, **these expenditures have been high structurally,** accounting for about 55 percent of subsector budget allocation in the middle of the 1980s in Francophone Africa (Orivel 1988 cited in Saint 1992, 48),[25] indicating a further fall of about 10 points in more than 20 years.

---

[25] In Anglophone African countries, the figure was approximately 12 percent.

Figure I.9: Structure of Public Unit Expenditure for Higher Education (excluding studies abroad) in Selected African Countries (most recent year available)

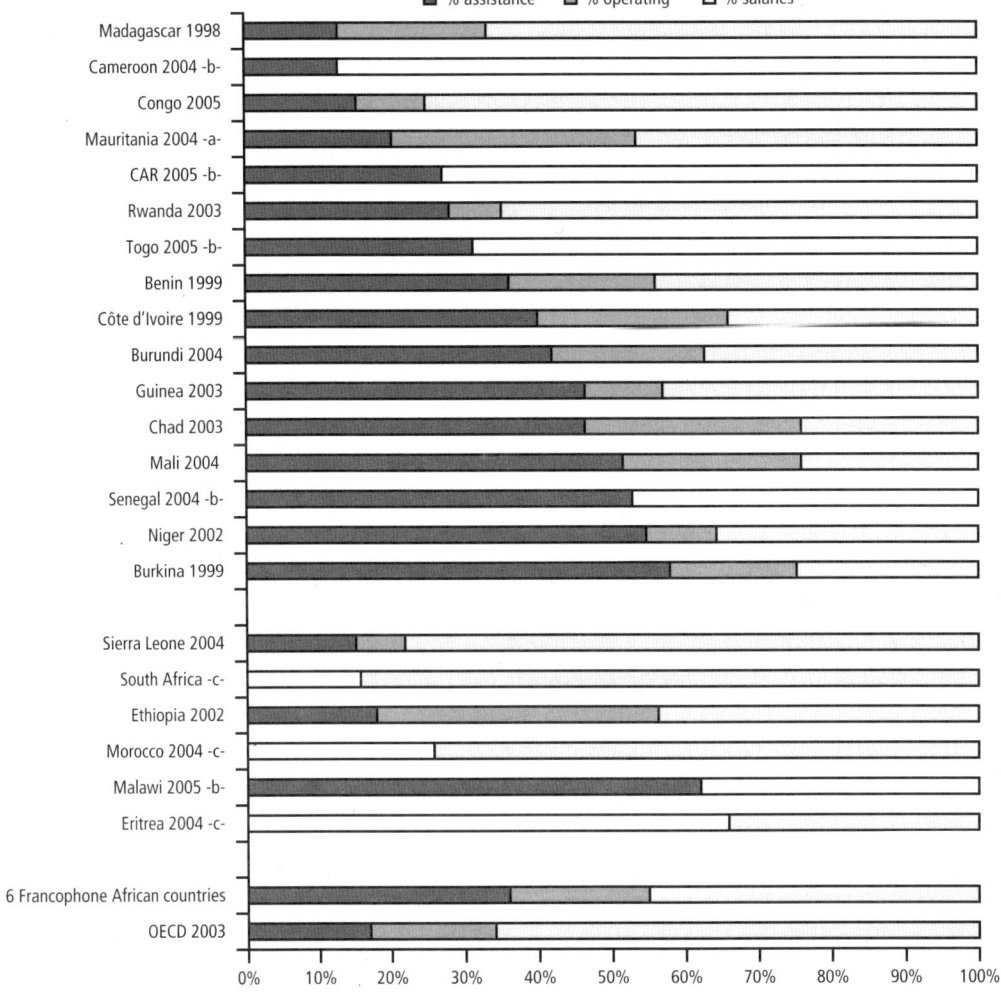

Sources: A number of RESEN and sector simulation models; UIS 2006b; OECD 2006; and authors' calculations. Data for the Central African Republic are estimates based on the 2005 and 2006 Finance Laws.
Note: OECD = Organisation for Economic Co-operation and Development.
a. Current expenditures are slightly underestimated with a bias for salaries.
b. Salaries and current expenditures were not separated.
c. Operating expenditures and social expenditures (USI data) were not separated.

Data on the provision of scholarships and loans to students as well as on assistance in kind (cafeteria, housing, transport, medical services, and so on) are scarce. For the countries for which data were obtained, however, **cash transfers account for about 65 percent[26] of social expendi-**

---

[26] This average was calculated taking into account eight countries: Benin, Central African Republic, Côte d'Ivoire, Guinea Conakry, Mauritania, the Republic of Congo, Rwanda, and

Table I.7: Summary on the Comparative Structure of Public Expenditures for Higher Education, most recent year available

Structure (%)	Low-income Francophone African countries		OECD 2003
	Excluding scholarships for studies abroad (%)	Including scholarships for studies abroad (%)	
Salaries	46	40	66
Variation	[24–70]	[14–58]	[43–80]
Operational expenditures	18	15	17
Variation	[6–33]	[4–29]	[6–52]
Social expenditures	36	45	17
Variation[a]	[13–58]	[13–70]	[2–43]
Total (%)	100	100	100
Percent of social expenditures for studies abroad in total current expenditures	n.a.	14	n.a.

Sources: OECD 2006; summary of previous analyses.
Note: OECD = Organisation for Economic Co-operation and Development; n.a. = not applicable.
a. Excluding countries with no, or negligible, social expenditures.

tures (excluding expenditures for studies abroad). There is a strong variation in these expenditures (see table I.7), however, because students in some countries receive barely any direct financial transfers (in Burundi and the Democratic Republic of Congo, for instance),[27] whereas half of the social expenditures in other countries is made up of scholarships (as is the case in Benin, Central African Republic, Côte d'Ivoire, Guinea Conakry, Mauritania, the Republic of Congo, and Senegal). Moreover, in certain countries, scholarships are provided in the form of loans (Rwanda, in particular). In OECD countries, the proportion of social aid granted to students in the form of loans rose from about 30 percent at the end of the 1990s to more than 40 percent in 2003 (OECD-UIS 2002; OECD 2006). In European Union countries, it was estimated at 36 percent in 2002 (Schmidt 2005). **The OECD countries giving out the highest level of public assistance to students are those offering student loans.** Often, governments tend to implement a system of student loans to reduce the costs involved in developing their higher education (OECD 2006, 255).

Expenditures for studies abroad account on average for 14 percent of the total budget allocated for higher education in 10 of the Francophone

---

Senegal. With the inclusion of Burundi (see note below), the average falls to 57 percent. By comparison, direct transfers to students account for only 3 percent of social expenditures in Ethiopia.

[27] In Burundi, all social expenditures are made by the organization in charge of university aid.

Figure I.10: Proportion of the Higher Education Current Budget Taken Up by Scholarships for Studies Abroad in Selected African Countries (percent)

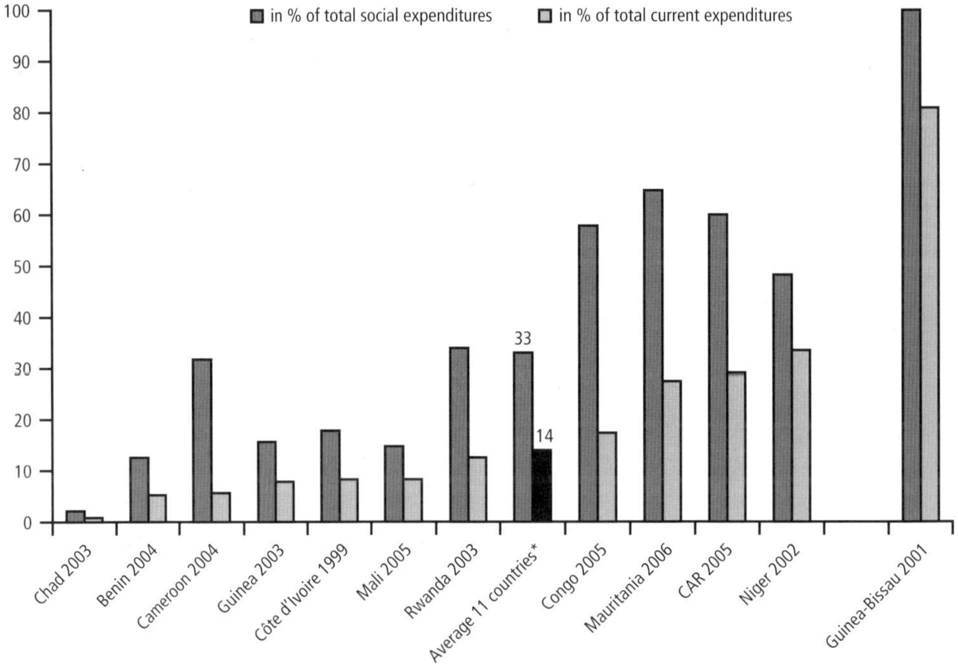

Sources: RESEN sector analyses and sector simulation models; Pôle de Dakar 2003; and authors' calculations. Data for the Central African Republic are estimates based on the 2005 and 2006 Finance Laws.
Note: This average does not include Guinea-Bissau. When including the latter, it rises to 20 and 38 percent, respectively.

African countries for which data are available. The range of variation is, however, significant with an allocation of less than 10 percent in Benin, Cameroon, Chad, Côte d'Ivoire, Guinea Conakry, and Mali, and of more than 10 percent in Central African Republic, Mauritania, Niger, the Republic of Congo, and Rwanda. Figure I.10 combines this data and highlights the particular case in Guinea-Bissau,[28] which has more students abroad than in its national institutions,[29] and for which social expenditures account for about 80 percent of public funds earmarked for higher education.

The public unit cost of subsidized education abroad is double that of education in national institutions.[30] This statement should, however, be interpreted with caution since the data are fragmentary (though certainly

---

[28] In 2001, this country had about 34 students per 100,000 inhabitants.
[29] The outward mobility rate (number of students abroad as a proportion of number of students in the country) is estimated at 122.4 percent according to UNESCO (see UIS 2006b).
[30] This average is calculated based on Cameroon, Mauritania, Niger, and Rwanda, using available data on the average unit cost of studies abroad.

underestimated). Studies abroad are usually undertaken for the following reasons:

Higher education training programs offered locally are limited (for instance, training in high technology sectors); lack desire to open up to the rest of the world; or the country's size is such that such training programs cannot be provided at a reasonable cost. A recent study by the UNESCO Institute of Statistics (UIS 2006b) points out that students from Sub-Saharan Africa are the most mobile in the world: 1 in every 16 students in the region studies in a foreign country.[31]

II.2.2.2. Do scholarships contribute to equity?

Assistance is used not only to encourage students to pursue higher education, but also to assist those with limited means to do so.

The *incentive argument* made sense at a time when graduates were too scarce (particularly during the period just after certain countries achieved independence), but it is no longer valid in many countries today, as shown by most empirical analyses on the external efficiency of higher education. In this respect, assistance to students today encourages the overproduction of individuals holding qualifications. To justify the production of graduates who do not have qualifications that are aligned with employment prospects in the modern sector of the economy, some have used the argument of high-productivity self-employment. This argument, however, has shown its limits in many countries. In Senegal, Foko, Ndém, and Reuge (2004) demonstrated that university graduates who work in the informal sector (20 percent of such degree holders) do not have a higher level of productivity than other individuals working in the sector that hold a high school diploma. Similar results were observed in the Republic of Congo in 2005 (25 percent of workers with university-level education work in the informal sector and their productivity is only marginally superior to that of high-school level graduates). Between 1991 and 1999 in Madagascar, scholarships were still being provided to encourage students to take up literary course programs, even though the principal avenue for employment in these fields of study, the public service, had run dry (during that time, the proportion of scholarship beneficiaries went up from 43 to 69 percent).

Regarding the *equity argument*, figure I.11 presents the findings of analyses carried out on household survey data. Although these comparisons should be taken with caution, as the sampling methods and definitions are not identical for all the countries, this graph suggests that youths

---

[31] That is 5.6 percent of students (see UIS 2006b, 37).

from privileged social classes are by far overrepresented in higher education. **Consequently, public higher education expenditure is largely skewed in favor of the richer.** On average, among the 10 countries surveyed, an individual belonging within the poorest 20 percent of households is 15.2 times less likely to pursue higher education than a person within the richest 20 percent of households (compared with 5.1 times less likely for secondary education, and 1.5 times less likely for primary education).[32] Thus, the majority of poor students quit school at the primary and secondary education level, raising the question of why scholarships are provided only to students pursuing higher education. According to Amelewonou and Brossard (2005), **current scholarship policies do not help the most impoverished pursue higher education.**

II.2.2.3. Salary costs vary from one country to the other

Salary costs account for an average of 45 percent of the public unit cost of higher education in the 15 countries for which data are available (see table I.8), and this varies from 24 to 70 percent depending on the country (factor of one to three). The faculty wage bill (for those occupying teaching positions) accounts for about two-thirds of total salary costs (comparable with OECD countries). This implies that the wage bill for nonteaching staff accounts for about one-third of total salary costs. Additionally, estimates suggest that a quarter of nonteaching staff salary costs goes to central or regional services staff, while the remaining third goes to the universities' administrative and technical staff. An important portion of the wage bill is reserved for various incentives (research incentives, supervision incentives, examination premiums, and so on), faculty overtime, and contingent teaching staff payments. These amounts that do not always fall under the salary heading must be added to the faculty wage bill. In the case of Mali, for instance, expenditures for overtime accounted for about 17 percent of expenditures for the teaching staff of the University of Bamako in 2004.[33]

Table I.8 shows that the situation varies from one country to another when it comes to the structure of salary costs. Unit costs can be relatively high for nonteaching staff in some countries, as is the case in the Democratic Republic of Congo, Madagascar, and Mauritania. This may well also be the case in Rwanda and Togo, given the rather high proportion of nonteaching staff in public higher education institutions. The average higher

---

[32] This result was recently confirmed by analyses carried out by Mingat (2006) on 26 Sub-Saharan African countries.

[33] The calculations were performed using RESEN Mali data.

Figure I.11: Differences at Each Level of Education between Pupils/Students Belonging to the Richest 20 Percent of the Population and Pupils/Students Belonging to the Poorest 20 Percent of the Population

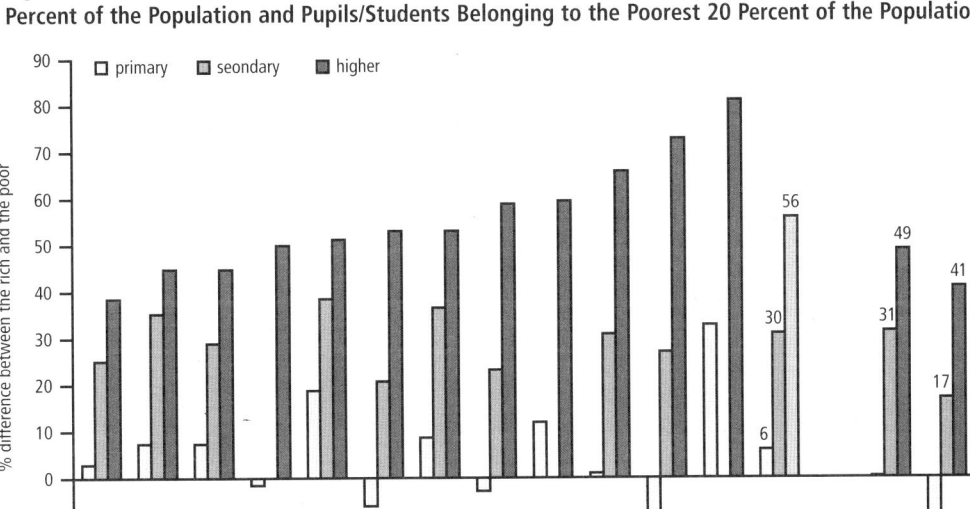

Sources: Davoodi, Tiongson, and Asawanuchit (2003) for 1990; UNESCO-Breda 2005; and RESEN analyses for the other countries.
Note: *The estimates for higher education in these countries cover all postprimary levels depending on the level of accuracy of available data.
For a given level of education, a difference of 0 indicates equal opportunities in school attendance for individuals belonging to the richest and poorest families. A negative difference indicates a lower participation of the richest (which is hardly observed after the primary term). A positive difference indicates a greater participation of the richest, and the more so as the difference moves up to 100.

education salary varies significantly from one country to another and although the estimate from available data for the 10 African countries puts this average at 14 times the per capita GDP on average, it tends to vary by a factor of one to nine, depending on the country.

II.2.2.4. The share of pedagogic expenditures in public education spending is low

Operating expenses (for instructional and noninstructional education institutions) account for about 20 percent of public expenditure per student in the 11 Francophone African countries for which data are available. In the four countries (Burkina Faso, Burundi, Madagascar, Mali) for which the available data enable a breakdown into instructional and noninstructional (central and decentralized administrative services) expenditures, it is estimated that nearly a quarter (24 percent) of overall current expendi-

Table I.8: Unit Salary Cost in Public Higher Education and Its Structure, in Selected African Countries, 1998–2004

Country | year	Salary unit cost as percent of public unit cost	Distribution of salary expenditures (%) Teaching staff	Distribution of salary expenditures (%) Nonteaching staff Institutions	Distribution of salary expenditures (%) Nonteaching staff Central administration[e]	Nonteaching staff unit cost (at institutions) in percent salary unit cost (institution)	Average salary (per capita GDP), at institutions only Teaching staff	Average salary (per capita GDP), at institutions only Nonteaching staff	Context: percent of nonteaching staff in the personnel (at institutions)
Benin 1999	44	75	25[a]	[a]	25[c]	15.5	—	55
Burkina 1999	45	64	25	11	28	—	—	71
Burundi 2004	37	64	34	2	34	37.2	8.0	55
Côte d'Ivoire 1999	34	75	19	6	20	12	2.5	47
Rep. of Congo 2005	75	66	32	2	33	11.9	6.5	40
Guinea Conakry 2003	43	75	6	19	7	10.3	1.2	80
Madagascar 1998	58	49	48	3	50	12.8	3.1	39
Mali 2004	24	87	13[a]	[a]	10	12.1	5.3	61
Mauritania 2004	41	54	34	12	38	9.0	3.5	61
Niger 2002	36	94[b]	[b]	6	—	—	—	61
Dem. Rep. of Congo 2002	—	—	—	—	54	4.1	3.0	29
Rwanda 1999	65	89[b]	[b]	11	—	—	—	73
Chad 2003	24	72	28[a]	[a]	28[c]	13.8	8.3	72
Togo 1999	—	—	—	—	—	—	—	—
Ethiopia 2002	44	53	37	10	41	27.1	7.9	54
Malawi 2001	34	70	30[a]	[a]	30[c]	24.7	—	78
Mozambique 1998	—	—	—	—	—	—	—	—
Sierra Leone 2004	78	—	—	—	—	—	—	67
Francophone Africa average	**43**	**68**	**25**	**8**	**30**	**13.9**	**4.6**	**55**
All countries average	45	67	25	8	31	15.9	4.9	59
OECD 2003	66	64	—	36[a]	—	—	—	—

Sources: RESEN sector analyses and complementary estimates; OECD-UIS (2005, table 2.7) for OECD.

Note: GDP = gross domestic product; OECD = Organisation for Economic Co-operation and Development; — = not available.

a. The figures in the "Institutions" column actually represent all the nonteaching staff in the institutions. The wage bill for the administrative staff in the institutions is on average three times that of the central services staff (average for seven countries).

b. The figures in the "Teaching staff" column represent all the teaching and nonteaching staff in the institutions. The teaching staff wage bill is on average twice that of the nonteaching staff of the institutions (average for seven countries).

c. This includes the central services staff's salary cost (this cost account for 10 percent of the total salary cost).

d. Average for public and private institutions.

e. "Central Administration" may also include regional services.

tures are directed to the subsector management (including both administrative and pedagogic activities). The remaining 76 percent is mainly utilized within the institutions for the purchase of goods and services, including education materials. The major part of current expenditures generally goes to the payment of utility bills (water, electricity, telephone, Internet, and so on), the hiring of security and maintenance personnel, and allowances for travel and fuel. In some cases, faculty overtime is often found here rather than in the wage bill.[34] Thus, the share of pedagogic expenditures is actually much smaller than it might seem.

Based on the above estimates, 16 percent of unit expenditure (that is, from 20 to 76 percent) is allocated for pedagogic expenditures in the higher education institutions of Francophone African countries.[35] An average statistic of 13 percent is obtained when the part for pedagogic expenditures is measured as a proportion of the overall sector budget (including scholarships and other assistance provided for studies abroad). This proportion is rather small when compared with the average for OECD countries (16 percent in 2003) or for a low-income African country like Ethiopia (35 percent). In real figures, this share is definitely small, particularly when considering that it must provide not only for the purchase of customary operating goods and services, but also for the financing of research activities[36] or the faculty's continuing education. Based on estimates made by the Association of African Universities, Saint (1992, 103) suggested that a university should direct a minimum of about 20 percent of its budget toward such activities if it is to maintain acceptable quality.

II.2.2.5. In some countries, hyperspecialization of institutions and relatively low student-teacher ratios contribute to the costliness of higher education

The breakdown of public unit costs (see box 2) highlights the low student-teacher ratios (the average number of students per teacher). Everything being equal, the lower the student-teacher ratio, the higher the unit cost. It is difficult to make these estimates, particularly given that nonpermanent and fixed-term teaching staff have to be accounted for in the cal-

---

[34] For the purpose of analysis, the budget allocation for overtime is included in salary expenditures.

[35] From what has been said before, this is a high estimate of the actual proportion of pedagogic expenditures in the current expenditures of higher education in Francophone African countries.

[36] In most African countries, the share of the higher education budget allocated for research activities is very low and highly dependent on external sources of funding—that is, more than 75 percent, for some 15 universities with available data (Saint 1992, 25, 51). This remains the case even today. For instance, in 1999, the transfer of funding to research insti-

culations.[37] This is made more difficult because of the lack of information on the respective teaching time (whether actual, preferably, or statutory) for permanent and nonpermanent teaching staff in most of the countries considered in this study. Student-teacher ratios calculated only on permanent teaching staff are thus overestimated (and probably largely so), given the high proportion of nonpermanent teaching staff in higher education institutions. The estimates provided here, although useful, are indicative and must be interpreted with caution (see figure I.12).

In the score of African countries with available data, the average student-teacher ratio is 23:1 in public higher education institutions (slightly higher in Francophone countries, with 25 students per 1 teacher). Student-teacher ratios, however, have slowly increased since the late 1980s when they averaged 14:1 for Sub-Saharan African countries as a whole (and 16 students per 1 teacher in the Francophone countries).[38] This indicates that, **although in some countries progress has been made in optimizing the size of amphitheaters, in others, teaching conditions have deteriorated.** By comparison, the 2004 student-teacher ratio in OECD countries was slightly less than 16:1 (OECD 2006). A comparison of these figures must consider the teaching staff's qualification structure, however, most notably because research management is critical for the development of quality higher education (see box 3).

In many countries, the variations of student-teacher ratios across institutions and education streams (a ratio of 1:10) are much more significant than cross-country variations (a ratio of 1:5) as shown in figure I.12. Appendix table B5 illustrates this particularly well for the Central African Republic, Madagascar, and Rwanda. Student-teacher ratios are generally higher in education streams such as law and social sciences; they are also higher in public universities than in specialized institutions. In this respect, the existence in many countries of highly specialized institutions (quite often with course programs disconnected from the actual demand of the labor market) generates high unit costs. Because of the strong growth of higher education systems (which will certainly continue in upcoming years, see Part Two of this study), physical capacity is already a major issue. In the Democratic Republic of Congo, for instance, the num-

tutions (as well as to some cultural institutions) accounted for only 0.11 percent of public current expenditures for higher education in Rwanda, while in Mali and Madagascar, the figure was 5 percent in 2004 and 8.3 percent in 1998, respectively (these figures are based on the authors' calculations using RESEN sectoral analyses).

[37] The number of permanent teachers must be converted into a number of full-time equivalent permanent teachers: that is, what is referred to as *full-time equivalent conversion.* When possible, full-time and part-time students should be accounted for separately.

[38] Figures for the end of the 1980s are estimates from data taken from Saint (1992, 65).

Figure I.12: Diversity of Student-Teacher Ratios in Public Higher Education Institutions in Selected African Countries (most recent year available)

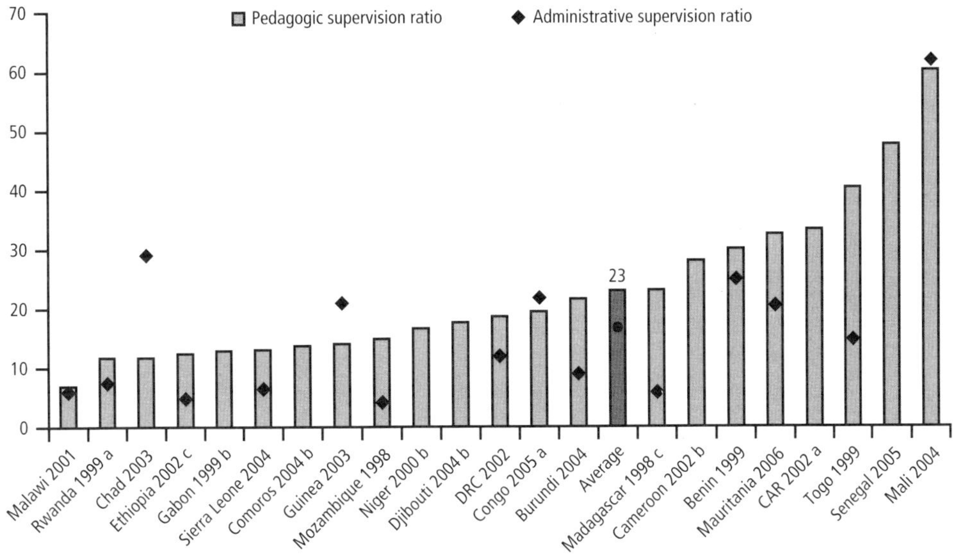

Sources: UIS; RESEN sector analyses and national data (Central African Republic, the Republic of Congo, and Senegal); authors' calculations.

Note:

a. The estimates only consider permanent teaching staff (57 percent of the teaching staff in the Republic of Congo and 22 percent in the Central African Republic).

b. USI data.

c. The estimates only consider national permanent teaching staff. For Chad, fixed-term staff (39 percent of the overall teaching personnel) were converted into the full-time equivalent and included. The student-teacher ratio only considers teaching staff holding actual teaching positions (not those without active teaching duties): some teachers carry out administrative duties (at the deanship, board of education, ministry, and so on) and are often exempt from teaching duties (they were taken into consideration in the calculation of the administrative supervision ratio).

ber of students in public institutions in Kinshasa in 2000 (89,000, or 61 percent of enrollments in public higher education institutions) was more than twice the number of slots theoretically available given the physical capacity (estimated at 40,000 in 2000).

II.2.3. Comparison of the structure of public expenditures for higher education to that in the other education levels

Table I.9 compares average public unit expenditures in higher, primary, and secondary education, using a sample of African countries for which data were available.

Table I.9 illustrates the factors determining the relative costliness of public higher education in Africa[39] compared with the other levels of education. These include higher student-teacher ratios, higher teaching staff

---

[39] This costliness is illustrated by data presented in appendix table B4.

BOX 3. STUDENT-TEACHER RATIOS DO NOT REFLECT THE TEACHING STAFF'S QUALIFICATIONS, OR THE DISTRIBUTION OF STUDENTS ACROSS THE VARIOUS UNIVERSITY COURSE PROGRAMS

On average, depending on the size of the higher education institutions or on the various course programs that they offer (see appendix table B5), the student-teacher ratios calculated here give out an idea of the average number of teaching staff in public universities, and enable cross-institution and cross-program comparisons, assuming that the relative teaching time (based on teachers' teaching hours per week) compared with the students' learning time is stable across course programs. The information used is essentially of a quantitative nature (which institution or course program has less teaching staff relative to the number of enrolled students?), and even when it provides insight in terms of costs, it does not shed any light: (i) on the cross-institution and cross-program distributions of enrolled students, and even less (ii) on the capacity of institutions to develop research activities (even if the number of teaching staff is sufficient), and (iii) on the training of postgraduate students (to ensure the next generation of teachers). Another drawback is that these ratios do not indicate the teachers' actual teaching hours.

Regarding the last two points, it should be noted that many Francophone African countries face both a quantitative issue—high levels of noninstructional staff and insufficient levels of instructional staff (see table I.7)—and a qualitative issue—teachers insufficiently qualified to train future senior researchers needed to conduct basic research. For instance, in Madagascar and the Democratic Republic of Congo, teachers attaining grades of professor or *"professeur titulaire"* full professor make up only 17 percent of the overall faculty. In Rwanda, barely 25 percent of the teaching staff have defended a doctorate thesis (while about half have attained a master's level at the very most). Moving to the west of the continent, to the two major public universities of Senegal (Cheik Anta Diop in Dakar, and Gaston Berger in Saint-Louis), only about 10 percent of the teaching staff have attained the professorial grade (AfDB Senegal 2006). Thus, an expansion of quality higher education systems will require not only increasing the number of teachers but also improving the qualification structure, notably the number of fully qualified lecturers.

Regarding the distribution of students across course programs, it should be remembered that if the numbers of students may be similar across course programs, the academic or professional profiles may be different. In fact, for a given unit cost level, such distribution can more or less vary based on the employment opportunities on the job market. In the more specific case of jobs offered in the education sector, this distribution is usually more or less in line with the needs for secondary school teachers. In fact, a recent study the UNESCO Institute of Statistics (see UIS 2006a) underlines that whereas in most countries some level of higher education is usually required to teach at the upper-secondary level, some countries still lack teachers with such qualification. This study points out Benin, Comoros, Ghana, and Uganda, where less than half of secondary school teachers have attained a minimum level of higher education (the proportion being 33 percent, 45 percent, 32 percent, and 42 percent, respectively, for these countries).

Table I.9: Modes of Organization at Different Education Levels in Sub-Saharan Africa, Averages and Variations in a Sample of 16–17 Low-Income Countries, 1998–2004 (public institutions only)

Level of education		Student-teacher ratio	Percent of nonteaching staff (institutions)	Average teaching staff salary (per capita GDP)	Percent of current expenditures excluding teaching staff salaries
Primary	Average	56	9	4,6	27,4
	Variation	[40–75]	[2–18]	[2,4–6,8]	[15–43]
Lower secondary	Average	37	—	6,6	37,4
	Variation	[23–56]	—	[3,6–13,1]	[24–56]
Upper secondary	Average	26	—	9,3	39,5
	Variation	[15–48]		[3,8–19,8]	[18–53]
Secondary	Average	33	27	—	—
	Variation	—	[5–52]	—	—
Higher education	Average	23	59	16,7	72
	Variation	[7–60]	[29–80]	[4,1–37,2]	[52–89]

Sources: Estimates for 16 low-income countries in Sub-Saharan Africa (percent of nonteaching staff and data for higher education); Mingat (2004) for other data (17 low-income countries of Sub-Saharan Africa, 1999–2003).
Note: GDP = gross domestic product; — = not available.

salaries (given the higher level of qualification that must be attained by higher education teachers), considerably higher proportion of social expenditures, and high levels of nonteaching staff in public higher education institutions—administrative supervision ratios (that is, the student-to-noninstructional staff ratio) are usually better than student-teacher ratios as shown in figure I.12.[40] In Francophone Africa, more than half of the staff of public higher education institutions is made up of administrative and technical staff (a figure that varies by a factor of 1 to 2.5 depending on the country). By comparison, in 2004, this proportion was about 40 percent in France.

In general, public higher education is more costly in Francophone Africa and this poses a problem for the quantitative growth of the systems. Budgets are largely skewed toward social expenses that fail to target the poorest, leaving few resources for academic and research activities. Cross-country variation of per student expenditure, both in terms of its level and structure (relative importance of the different components), indicates that **different policies were implemented, which in turn means that efficiency gains and a better equilibrium between academic and social expenditures are possible,** resulting in a more enabling environment for quality education.

II.3. DIFFERENTIATING UNIT EXPENDITURE BY TYPE OF INSTITUTION[41]

II.3.1. Public expenditure per student varies across institutions

Fixed costs in public higher education institutions are significant because of the high number of administrative and technical staff as well as to the type of course programs and degrees. In the same institution, some course programs, such as literary, law, and economics undergraduate programs, are likely to be overcrowded with student-teacher ratios generally above 80, whereas enrollment is usually low in programs such as science or even graduate or postgraduate literary course programs, with student-teacher ratios as low as 4:1 or 5:1 and a high public expenditure per student.

Table I.10 compares unit expenditure in public universities and in other postsecondary public institutions. It shows that costs in public post-

---

[40] The proportion of nonteaching staff in the overall personnel of higher education institutions is by far higher than the calculated proportion in primary- and secondary-cycle institutions. At the primary and secondary level, nonteaching staff members are often found in administration (central or regional) unlike what prevails in higher education.

[41] The differentiation presented here is simply indicative (as it is more pertinent to compare costs between institutions offering services of a similar nature). Although it indicates that some course programs or training programs are more expensive than others, it is important to consider how pertinent the course programs are when it comes to the job market or to the country's development.

Table I.10: Comparison of the Public Unit Training Cost in Public Universities and in Other Postsecondary Public Institutions in Selected Countries

Country	year	Average unit cost of the other institutions as a multiple of that of universities	Students of the "other" institutions		Public institutions compared
		as a percent of the number of students at universities	as a percent of the total in higher education	
					Extended course of studies
Institutes and higher schools of learning				
Madagascar 1999[a]	3.4	17	10	Higher schools of learning and institutes managed by universities
Mali 2004	1.9	13	12	Higher schools of learning and higher education institutes
Rwanda 2001	1.4	58	21	Kigali Institute of Science, Technology and Management; Kigali Institute of Health; Higher Institute of Agronomy and Livestock
Training of teaching staff				
Burundi 2004	0.6	23	13	Higher Teacher Training College (ENS)
Madagascar 1999	4.1	5	3	ENS and ENS for technical education
Mauritania 2004	1.4	21	15	ENS and Teacher Training College for school teachers
Mozambique 1998	0.5	23	18	Pedagogic Institute
Niger 1998	10.2 (2.2)[b]	1 (8)[b]	1 (8)[b]	ENS
				Short course of studies
Madagascar 1999	4.2	2	1	Professional Training Institute (Higher Institute of Technology, two-year training programs)

Distance learning	Average cost of distance learning as a multiple of unit cost on campus	Distance learning enrollment as a percent of the total number of students in higher education	Distance Learning Center (DLC) concerned[d]
Madagascar 1999	0.10 (0.7)[c1]	26 (103)[c2]	National Distance Learning Center of Madagascar (CNTEMAD)
China	0.2–0.4	24	—
France	0.5	2	Interuniversity Distance Learning Federation
India	0.4	11	*Indira Gandhi National Open university*
Indonesia	0.13	18	*Universitas Terbuka*
Ireland	0.4–0.7	5	*National Centre for Distance Education*
Japan	0.13	4	*University of the Air*
Malaysia	0.73	3	*Universiti Sains*
Pakistan 1988	0.22	—	*Allama Iqbal Open University*
United Kingdom	0.4–0.5	8	*Open university*
Thailand	0.4	37	*Open university*
11-country average[e]	0.3–0.4	4	—

Sources: RESEN sector analyses for African countries and complementary estimates; World Bank (1994) for Pakistan; Saint (1999), Daniel (1996), and Dhanarajan (1994) for the other countries.

Note: — = not available.

a. The National School of Computer Technology (ENI) also hands out intermediate certificates after two years of studies.

b. The figures in parentheses are for 1990. Between 1990 and 1998, the number of students enrolled in ENS fell by two-thirds.

c1. The figure in parentheses relates the number of students enrolled at the National Distance Learning Center of Madagascar (CNTEMAD) to that of the School of Law, Economics, Management, and Sociology (DEGS), which provides similar learning programs but in a different form.

c2. The figure in parentheses relates CNTEMAD enrollment to that of the DEGS.

d. Of all these institutions, only those in Madagascar, Ireland, and Malaysia have fewer than 8,000 students.

e. This average is obtained for the data available on the 11 or 10 countries.

secondary institutions (specialized higher education institutes, higher schools of learning) are generally higher than in universities, as is the case in Burundi and Mozambique. Teacher-training colleges are not systematically costly, however. The relative costliness of an institution seems to be closely linked to its size, and institutions with a small number of enrolled students tend to have higher operating unit expenses (because of economies of scale).

Little information is available on public expenditure per student involved in distance learning programs in Francophone African countries. In theory, operating costs associated with distance learning should be lower than those associated with face-to-face learning: distance learning optimizes the student-teacher ratio and thus reduces salary costs, everything being equal.[42] This is usually the case as long as the number of students is sufficiently high and constant (Saint 1992, 108; Murphy, Anzalone, Bosch, and Moulton 2002, 33)[43] enough to amortize initial investments on staff training, curriculum development, preparation of education materials, and acquisition of the chosen technology (Saint 1999, 24). When these conditions are met, available data indicate that unit costs (public expenditure per student) in big distance learning centers average only 40 percent of those associated with face-to-face learning.

Distance learning can be used to improve on the overall quality of education. For instance, in Madagascar, where few students are involved in distance learning (fewer than 8,000 in 1999), the cost per degree holder is 25 percent less compared with those for the School of Law, Economics, Management, and Sociology (DEGS), which provides face-to-face education of the same nature.

In actuality, distance learning students are for the most part also enrolled in regular classes at university. Distance learning classes (in the form of photocopies) seem to be more of a complement to regular classes and hence improve the quality of the students' education. In this respect, some specialists point out that "the distance separating lecturers and stu-

---

[42] In Madagascar, for instance, there are 6 students per 1 nonteaching staff (administrative and technical staff) in the so-called classical public universities, whereas the number is 86 per 1 nonteaching staff at CNTEMAD (the National Distance Learning Center of Madagascar, according to 1999 data).

[43] Given the frequently high student dropout rate in distance learning universities (World Bank 1994, 34), although it is appropriate to compare costs per degree holder, it should be noted that distance learning students often strive to improve on their skill sets rather than ultimately obtain a degree, which is not reflected in the cost per degree holder (Murphy, Anzalone, Bosch, and Moulton 2002, 34). This said, in the case of Madagascar, it has been estimated that unit cost per degree holder for CNTEMAD (in 1999) was 0.75 times that of the School of Law, Economics, Management, and Sociology (DEGS). This result is similar to that posted in table I.10 (a unit cost of 0.7).

dents requires broader clarity, logical coherence and good organization of course presentation, thus increasing pedagogic efficiency. When long-distance learning courses are prepared by lecturers of the regular learning system, the quality of face-to-face learning is also improved" (Saint 1992, 20). Finally, distance learning can contribute to reduce study opportunity costs for working students (Saint 1999; Murphy, Anzalone, Bosch, and Moulton 2002) and could be an alternative to those whose physical conditions or status would not otherwise permit them to further their education.

II.3.2. Unit expenditure also varies with the field of study

The cost per student in public universities varies with the type of faculty and course of studies. Science and technology faculties that tend to utilize more expensive equipment and to enroll a limited number of students (see figure I.13) incur higher costs (see table I.11).

Many countries have introduced reforms to broaden their higher education course offerings. In Madagascar, for instance, the **introduc-**

Figure I.13: Distribution of Higher Education Students According to Course Programs for Selected Francophone African Countries (public institutions only)

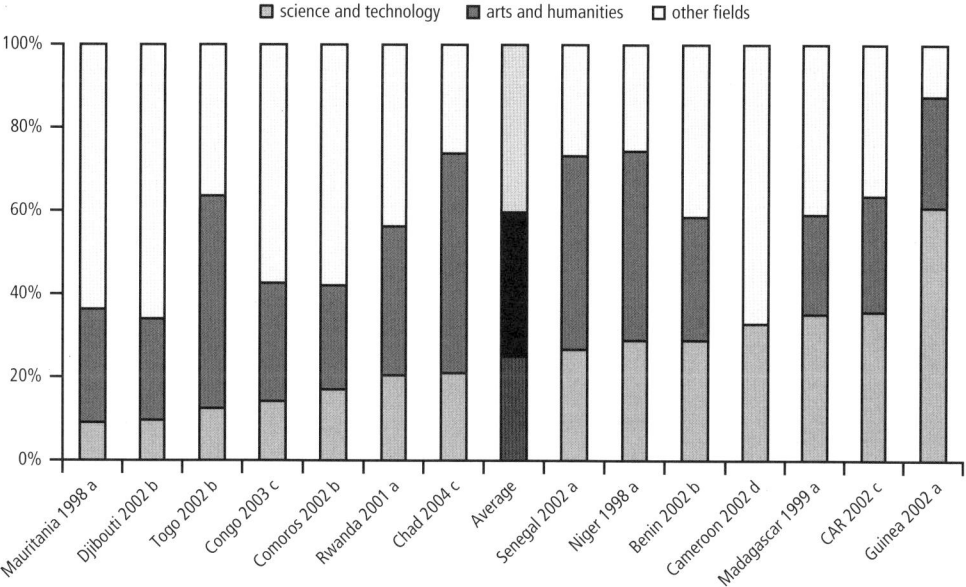

Sources: Estimates from various sources (RESEN sector analyses, UIS, national data).
Note:
a. Only university.
b. UIS data.
c. Universities, institutes, and higher schools of learning.
d. Only enrollment in "scientific" course programs is available.

Table I.11: Comparison of Public Unit Costs in Major Course Programs of Public Universities in Selected Countries

Country | year	Average unit cost of the course program as a multiple of the average unit cost at university		
	Scientific and technological programs	Literature and humanities	Social sciences, commerce, and law
Madagascar 1999[a]	1.01	1.9	0.44
Mauritania 1998	2.7	0.9	0.8
Niger 1999	1.8	0.5	0.44
Rwanda 2001	1.5	1.2	0.9
Chad 2004	1.9	0.8	0.7
Average[b]	1.8	1.1	0.6

Sources: RESEN, simulation models, and authors' estimates.
Note:
a. Madagascar has relatively fewer students in the art faculty (24 percent) than other countries (from 27 percent in Mauritania to 46 percent in Niger and 53 percent in Chad). Only university students are taken into account.
b. The interpretation is as follows: for the selected countries, unit costs of scientific programs in public institutions are on average 1.8 times higher than university unit costs, versus 0.76 times the university unit costs for other programs (humanities, social sciences, and others).

tion of preselection in regular university programs has reduced university intake rate from a base 100 percent to 56 percent in less than 10 years (between 1988 and 1998). In 1999, the faculties had enrolled only 58 percent of students compared with 92 percent in 1990. The share of students enrolled in higher schools of learning went up by 8 to 10 percent. In other countries, a rather significant proportion of students is enrolled in specialized higher education institutes (25 percent of students in Guinea Conakry, 33 percent in Rwanda[44]) or short higher education professional courses such as the University Degree in Technology (DUT) or Senior Technician Certificate (BTS) (23 percent in Senegal, 13 percent in Madagascar).[45] The private sector is capable of providing short professional training programs at low cost. In Côte d'Ivoire, for instance, in the early 1990s, BTS-type training programs in private institutions were eight times less costly than those in Yamoussoukro's *Grandes écoles* (public higher learning institutions). The state thus decided to turn to private institutions for this type of training programs instead. In Madagascar, in the mid-1990s, costs incurred per student in short professional course programs in the private sector were

---

[44] This figure does not consider the number of students in the Institute of Education Sciences of Kigali where 11 percent of the students in public higher education institutions are enrolled (2001 data).
[45] These figures are cited by Mazeran (2006).

about half of public unit cost in the *Instituts supérieurs de technologie* (tertiary-level institutes of technology offering short professional training programs). Yet such training programs are often better geared toward the job market and are better suited to meet the countries' development challenges.

Table I.11 shows that higher schools of learning and technological institutes are more costly than universities. However the reverse may be true when costs per degree holder are considered. Internal inefficiency (caused by repeater and dropout ratios) is indeed much higher in universities than in higher schools of learning (given the entry selection process in the latter).[46] The formulation of public policies for the financing of higher education must go beyond a comparison of unit costs by type of institution. Cost per degree holder, and more preferably cost per degree holder entering the job market, should be the principal parameter to consider. It is particularly important to develop information systems on degree holders (statistics on repeater, survival, and degree achievement rates; graduate career surveys; collection of employment data) with the aim of better orientating states' investment policy decisions.

III. LEVEL OF HOUSEHOLD CONTRIBUTIONS FOR HIGHER EDUCATION

The private financing of higher education can be provided by students or their parents, private profit-making (companies) or nonprofit entities (including nongovernmental organizations [NGOs], religious groups, and so on), and even by resources generated by the public or private learning institutions themselves.

In this section, only the direct participation of households in the funding of higher education will be analyzed.

---

[46] For instance, in the 1997–98 school year, the repeating rate was 20 percent in the universities of Madagascar, 16 percent in distance learning education, 1 percent in private institutions, and 2 percent in professional training institutes (ISTs). Furthermore, the dropout rate before the end of the first year of studies was about 37 percent in the universities, 40 percent in the faculty of medicine, 16 percent in higher schools of learning, 78 percent in distance learning education, and 8 percent in the ISTs. The continuation rates for the last year were estimated at only 26 percent in the universities, 33 percent in the faculty of medicine, 53 percent in the higher schools of learning, 5 percent in distance learning education, and 92 percent in the ISTs. Similar results were found in the higher education system of Rwanda in 2001 (33 percent dropout rate before the end of the first year at the national university, 40 percent before the end of the last year). Private institutions have a better internal efficiency.

Figure I.14: Students Enrolled in Private Institutions as a Percent of Total Higher Education Enrollment, in Selected Low-Income Countries

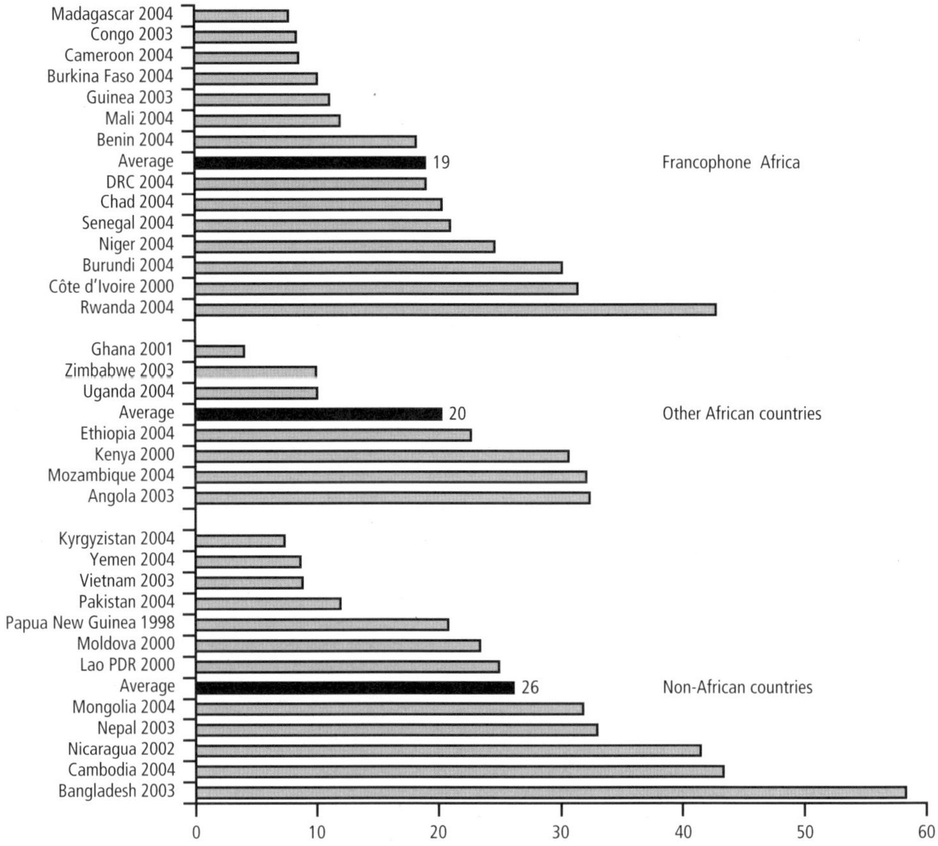

Sources: Appendix table B1; UIS 2006b; World Bank Edstats; RESEN.
Note: By comparison, in OECD countries, 30 percent of students tend not to complete their studies (OECD 2006). This figure is for 2004. The figure for Mauritius in 2003 is 18 percent.

III.1. IMPORTANT ROLE OF THE PRIVATE SECTOR IN HIGHER EDUCATION SERVICES OFFERING

On average, **one out of five students is enrolled in a private institution in Francophone Africa,** a proportion equivalent to the average for the other African countries (20 percent) but lower than the average for OECD countries (26 percent).

Figure I.14 illustrates a strong variation in the proportion of students enrolled in the private sector for some low-income countries (a factor of 1 to 15 between Ghana and Bangladesh). Among Francophone African countries, it ranges from 8 percent in Madagascar to 43 percent in Rwanda (a factor of one to five), without any relation to the country's level of economic development (in Cameroon, for instance, it is only 9 percent).

Other factors, particularly incentives given by the state to promote the development of the private sector, seem to have a major influence on the variation.

Furthermore, in contrast to what is generally the case worldwide,[47] higher education is less privatized than secondary education in most Francophone African countries (19 percent compared with 24 percent). Furthermore the privatization of primary education tends to be more important in countries where there is little privatized higher education. Countries with the highest share of public higher education funding appear to compensate for their lack of public resources to meet a soaring social demand for primary education with greater private ownership at this level. This said, the more privileged social classes are largely overrepresented in higher education, whereas at the low levels of the education system representation is more evenly balanced. This budget allocation policy in favor of higher education at the detriment of primary education threatens to engender or further worsen social inequality with respect to access to education.

III.2. OVERVIEW OF HOUSEHOLD EXPENDITURES ON HIGHER EDUCATION[48]

The **gross contribution**[49] made by households to the financing of higher education varies considerably, from less than 10 percent in Mali and the Republic of Congo to 72 percent in Rwanda. This contribution is 12 percent in Madagascar, 23 percent in Senegal, 26 percent in Mauritania, and 38 percent in Cameroon. On average these figures are relatively low, with the average value for these seven Francophone African countries being 25 percent compared with 44 percent in the other non-African countries (see table I.12).[50]

---

[47] Among most low-income countries, the average figures are 12, 18, and 22 percent for primary, secondary, and higher education, respectively (World Bank's *Edstats* data consulted in February 2006).

[48] Estimating education expenditures incurred by families is a difficult task because of the lack of data. Assessing these expenditures requires resorting to specific surveys to determine all the direct education costs incurred per student (registration fees, contributions to university associations, purchase of textbooks and supplies, transportation costs, housing expenses, and miscellaneous expenditures). This is a delicate exercise because expenditures induced directly in schooling should be distinguished from those related to it (see box 4). Additionally these data do not always enable a distinction between expenditures made in public institutions from those made in other types of institutions.

[49] In this estimate, it is assumed that households and the state are the only sources of funding for education. Thus, private expenditures are expressed as a percent of public current expenditures and these private expenditures.

[50] These are, for the most part, developing countries. In these countries of comparison, the gross contribution ranges from 20 percent in Jamaica to 80 percent in Chile.

Table I.12. Household Unit Expenditure for Higher Education in Selected Countries, 1999–2005 (excluding studies abroad)

| | Household average expenditures per higher education student | | | | |
| | Public and private institutions | | Public institutions | | Private institutions |
	Percent of public unit cost	Percent of per capita GDP	Percent of public unit cost	Percent of per capita GDP	Percent of per capita GDP
Francophone Africa					
Mali 2004	3	(< 0)	6	—	—	—
Rep. of Congo 2005	6	(< 0)	7	6	2	14
Madagascar 1999	12[a]	(1)	13[a]	5 [1–12][a]	5 [2–43][a]	86
Senegal 2001	23	(< 0)	49	—	—	—
Mauritania 2004	36	(13)	43	—	—	—
Cameroon 2001	55	(32)	47	39	33	100
Rwanda 2000	155[b]	(69)	150[b]	—	—	[137–237][a]
Dem. Rep. of Congo 2001[d]	—	—	—	[350–530][c]	[199–298][c]	—
Average	**41**	**(—)**	**45**	—	—	—
Other countries					
Ethiopia 2002[e]	11	(14)	124	—	—	—
Jamaica 1999	21	(19)				
Indonesia 1999	29	(48)				
Argentina 1999	32	(27)				
China 1999	33	(21)				
Jordan 1999	46	(35)				
Peru 1999	53	(46)				
Paraguay 1999	99	(49)				
Malaysia 1999	125	(8)				
Chile 1999	222	(73)				
Average non-Africa	**79**	**(36)**				
Average of other countries	67	(34)				
OECD 1999	50	(17)				

Sources: Estimates from Foko, Ndém, and Reuge 2004; RESENs; OECD-UIS 2002 sector analyses.

Note: OECD = Organisation for Economic Co-operation and Development; — = not available.

Countries are classified in increasing order of household unit expenditure in relation to public unit cost. Figures in parenthesis refer to the *net* contribution of households to higher education financing. Assuming that the state and households are the principal sources of finance for higher education, the net contribution of households refers to the household expenditures going to higher education (excluding social expenditures) as a percentage of the sum of public expenditures and household expenditures (excluding social expenditures to avoid double counting).

a. This refers only to registration fees. Its range of variation depending on the type of institution is indicated in brackets.

b. Tuition expenses account for 68 percent of higher education private expenditures.

c. This refers to a range of variation that depends on the level of expenditures other than tuition expenses.

d. Tuition expenses account for 50 to 75 percent of private expenditures of higher education in public universities.

e. This refers to registration fees for evening classes relative to per capita GDP or to the public operating unit cost of public institutions for day students.

Figure I.15: The Proportion of Pupils/Students Enrolled in Private Institutions in Selected Francophone African Countries, 2000–04 (most recent year)

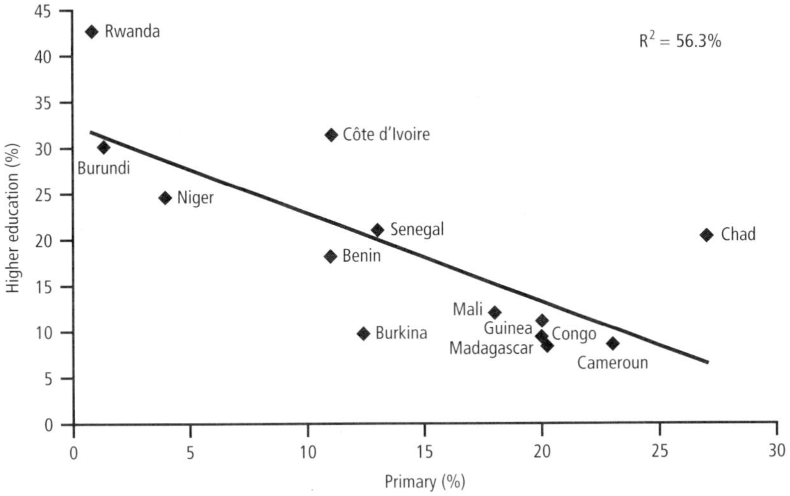

Sources: Appendix table B1; World Bank *Edstats.*

The **net contribution** of households (obtained by subtracting the social expenditures paid for by the state from the direct expenditures incurred by households based on estimates from household surveys) is 13 percent in Mauritania, 32 percent in Cameroon, and 69 percent in Rwanda. It is very low in Madagascar and negative in Mali, the Republic of Congo, and Senegal. This shows that the state is the main net source of funding to higher education in these countries and that cost-sharing strategies in public universities should be considered.[51] The net contribution of households to the financing of higher education is more significant in the non-African countries used in the comparison (36 percent), mainly because of their relatively low level of social expenditures compared with those in Sub-Saharan Africa.

Household expenditures on higher education are higher when they finance enrollment in private institutions. This is the case in Cameroon, the Republic of Congo, and Madagascar. This may also be the case for the other countries of the region as tuition expenses (the principal components of private expenditures) are higher in private institutions than in public institutions. The development of the private sector should be supported by financial assistance that adequately targets the most impoverished and underprivileged groups with the aim of curbing the worsening

---

[51] In the case of Mali, the Republic of Congo, and Senegal, household expenditures allocated for higher education account for 10 percent, 17 percent, and just below 50 percent, respectively, of social expenditures at this level of education.

problems of already considerable inequality and social mobility. In fact, the financial contributions made by households are not proportional to their standards of living because poor households generally tend to make a more substantial contribution considering their level of income (see box 5 on the case in Cameroon).

Finally, when it comes to the structure of private expenditures, the largest portion goes to tuition expenses (this account for about 68 percent in Rwanda and between 50 and 75 percent in the DRC) or textbook purchases (8 percent in Rwanda, between 15 and 47 percent in Cameroon, depending on the household's standard of living). The remaining expenditures (about 25 percent in Cameroon and Rwanda) go to related uses (transportation, rent, uniforms, Internet connection, etc.).

BOX 4: WHICH EXPENDITURE ITEMS SHOULD BE CONSIDERED WHEN ESTIMATING HOUSEHOLD EDUCATION EXPENDITURE?

The estimate of household education expenditure depends on how these expenditures are defined. Some expenditures arise directly from education, whereas others are only related to it. A third category is considered to be too far away from education to be included in education expenditure (though these expenditures can have a positive effect on student performance just like the expenditures from the two first categories). The first two categories of expenses, depending on data availability, can be identified by separating expenditures made to purchase textbooks and supplies from those for the payment of registration fees. The table below attempts this classification and is based on data from a 2001 household survey carried out in Cameroon.

Breakdown of the Education Expenditures for Assessment Purposes

	Direct expenditures	Related expenditures	Other expenditures
Textbooks and supplies	—Textbooks —Exercise books —Other study materials	—Uniforms	
Tuition expenses	—Registration fees —Parent Teacher Assocation contribution —Boarding fees —Room rent —Processing fees	—Other tuition expenses	
Other education expenditures		—Private tutoring —Home-based schooling —Cafeteria fees —School transport —Learning fees —Internet connection	—Arts education —Textbooks (not subject related) —Newspapers, magazines —Other materials

Learning fees refer to the expenditures made by families for their children involved in a learning program not under an education institution. For instance, payments made to a hairdresser for the training of a girl in hairdressing (without any registration in a course program leading to a hairdresser diploma). From the fam-

(*continues on the following page*)

BOX 4: (CONTINUED)

ilies' point of view, cafeteria fees arise because of schooling. It would, however, be appropriate to deduct from these expenditures the amount that, in any case, would have been spent to feed the pupils if they had not been taking their meals from the school. Thus, this is an education expenditure inflation factor for the families. These expenses might be viewed as not being compulsory, because it can be assumed that the student can bring his or her own food to school (in which case it is considered as a related expenditure). This is also the case for school transport expenses: the pupil/student could walk to school. Is transportation a luxury or an education expenditure? Here, too, the issue is far from being decided. And although uniforms are compulsory, the burden to purchase other clothes is lessened. In effectively estimating education expenditures, only those referring to the first two categories, direct and related expenditures, are to be considered. All the same, this is just an indication of how broad education expenditure could be perceived.

Source: RESEN Cameroon.

BOX 5: THE CASE OF CAMEROON: FINANCIAL EFFORT *REQUIRED* FROM POOR HOUSEHOLDS FOR THE FINANCING OF HIGHER EDUCATION IS CONSIDERABLE

In Cameroon, households contribute about 32 percent (net contribution) to the national expenditure for higher education. Such contribution is relatively high compared with other Francophone African countries for which data are available. In absolute terms, the poorest households spend less than the richest households (40 percent less, a difference that goes up when considering only expenditures in private institutions). However, **the biggest financial effort is made by the poor when educating their children beyond primary education:** private expenditure per student is 13 times higher than that for a child in primary education for a household within the poorest quintile, compared with 4 times higher for a household within the richest quintile.

Study materials, including university textbooks (which are priority expenditures), cut a much more significant portion of the higher education budget of poor households as compared with the rich households for whom tuition expenses take the largest portion (particularly those associated with housing). Interquintile differences in expenditures are low in public institutions but very high in private institutions (192,000 FCFA per poor household student compared with 535,000 FCFA per rich household student, or about three times more). Students from rich families tend to go to private institutions, which are on average more costly (and more prestigious), and spend a significant amount in related expenses (transportation and food in particular) as the budget coefficient associated with these related expenses (24 percent) is not low compared with that of poor students (26 percent).

In general, this indicates that **wealthier households are more able to finance their children's higher education (and the more so when it comes to private education).**

(continues on the following page)

BOX 5: (CONTINUED)

Household Higher Education Expenditures Relative to Their Quintile and the Type of Institution, 2001

	Households from the 20 percent poorest			Households from the 20 percent richest		
	Public	Private	Overall	Public	Private	Overall
Annual expenditure per student, in thousands of CFA	151	192	156	165	535	267
As a multiple of that for primary education	22	13	14	5	7	5
Structure (percent)						
Textbooks and supplies			47			15
Tuition expenses[a]			27			61
Related expenses[b]			26			24
Overall			100			100

Source: Authors' calculations from RESEN Cameroon.

Note: These data are coherent in indicating an average proportion of students in private institutions of about 20 percent, 12 percent among the poorest, and 28 percent among the richest. This average estimate from the household survey is higher than that obtained from education statistics (9 percent) but probably near to the case in reality.

a. Including expenses associated with room rent, student associations, and diverse administrative fees.

b. Transportation, cafeteria, and uniform expenses.

PART TWO

Perspectives for Developing Higher Education in Francophone Africa According to a Budgetary Sustainability Logic

This part identifies the constraints of and potential scope for developing higher education systems in Francophone Africa.

The first part of this study demonstrated how in many of these countries financing the quantitative expansion of higher education was implicitly done by decreasing public expenditure per student. Because salaries and public assistance were rather stable over time, this decrease has been translated in many countries by an increase of the teacher-student ratio and a decrease in spending on instructional material or funds allocated to research, which are both key elements for ensuring quality. Although these decreases in spending and increases in ratios do not explain everything, poor teaching conditions certainly constitute one of the reasons behind the overall ineffectiveness of Francophone higher education, from the internal standpoint (significant dropout and retention rates) and that of graduates entering into the labor market.

Moreover, in many countries, **current trends are not financially sustainable.** Because neither governments nor external aid can make higher education a top priority (most Francophone African countries are still far from achieving UPC goals), the budgetary constraints will be difficult to overcome, with few exceptions. Plans to develop higher education systems must, in the majority of Francophone countries, offer better mid-

and long-term balance than currently in force, which most often stems from the systems themselves, not from proactive policies. Seeking such balance between social demand and quality and efficiency requirements while taking equity into account must be achieved by way of technical efforts led on a national level to assess the various quantitative and qualitative options to expand a long-term higher education development plan that is socially feasible and financially sustainable.

This study does not propose an exhaustive list of solutions for meeting this goal. It does, however, seek to clarify the feasibility of certain development options by using financial simulation models that make it possible to estimate the cost of various policy scenarios. These policy scenarios offer original perspectives via either their quantitative objectives—that is, the means of providing services—or the capacity to rely more or less on private financing. We first will analyze the demand for higher education, country by country, on the 2015 horizon. We then will perform financial simulations of the different implications of policy options, both on the level of mobilizing public and private resources for higher education and on methods of providing services. Last, we will determine the portion of the demand that may be effectively educated.

I. EXPANDING SYSTEMS ON THE BASIS OF CURRENT POLICIES IS NOT FINANCIALLY SUSTAINABLE

The first simulation evaluates the financial sustainability of expanding higher education and assumes that the following remain unchanged: student flow management, intra- and intersectoral budgetary allotments, criteria for granting scholarships and their amounts, staff recruitment, and teacher salaries.

I.1. A HIGH SOCIAL DEMAND THAT SHOULD CONTINUE TO GROW[52]

The coverage of all levels of education has significantly increased since 1990. Among them, quantitative progress has been the most significant at the postprimary levels throughout the last 15 years in Africa. On average for the entire continent, between 1990 and 2004, the primary school

---

[52] The term "social demand" simply refers to the number of students effectively accounted for in enrollment statistics or the number projected for the next 10 years. As estimated here, it still does not include the potential number of candidates enrolling in higher education. In effect, certain countries have introduced a selection process for entering university (as in the case of Niger), which can limit enrollment numbers.

completion rate went from 49 percent to a little more than 60 percent, and the enrollment rates in secondary school greatly improved or practically doubled: for the lower-secondary level, the rate has gone from 35 to 48 percent; for the upper-secondary level, the rate increased from 14 to 26 percent. These significant changes in the number of students enrolled in the preuniversity levels have resulted in a practically automatic, similar increase in enrollment rates in higher education: the average number of students per 100,000 inhabitants in low-income African countries increased from 164 to 441 between 1990 and 2004. Put differently, **the social demand for higher education has greatly increased and the systems have responded positively** by absorbing rising numbers of students into higher education.

The Francophone countries are no exception to this general trend observed on the African continent. The average annual growth of the number of students increased by 8 percent between 1991 and 2002, and by 9 percent between 2000 and 2004. In certain countries, social demand is booming. For example, between 1991 and 2004, the annual growth rate was 13 percent in Mauritius, 15 percent in Mali, 16 percent in Côte d'Ivoire, 18 percent in Rwanda, and 19 percent in the Comoros. In some countries, this progress was facilitated by increased private sector offerings. Although private initiatives to create higher education institutions were practically nonexistent in Francophone Africa in the 1990s (World Bank 2002), today an average of 20 percent of students are enrolled in a private institution, reaching 25 percent in some countries (Burundi, Côte d'Ivoire, Niger, and Rwanda).

As long as the primary and secondary levels of education continue growing significantly over the years to come, so too will the fast growth rate of the social demand for higher education. Three projections of this demand were calculated and are presented in figure II.1.

- In the *first projection*, we linearly projected the number of students enrolled by 2015 based on the trends observed between 1991 and 2004. This projection results in around 1.1 million students in 2015 in all of the Francophone countries. This projection, however, does not account for the most recent development of higher education systems. Indeed, student enrollment increased more in the 2000s than in the 1990s.
- Hence, a *second projection* was performed based on the most recent trends (those occurring between 2000 and 2004). Should student enrollment continue growing at this rate, approximately 1.4 million students would be enrolled in 2015 throughout Francophone Africa, or double the cur-

Figure II.1: Trends in Enrollment Since 1980 and Projected Social Demand, 2004–15 (21 countries in Francophone Africa)

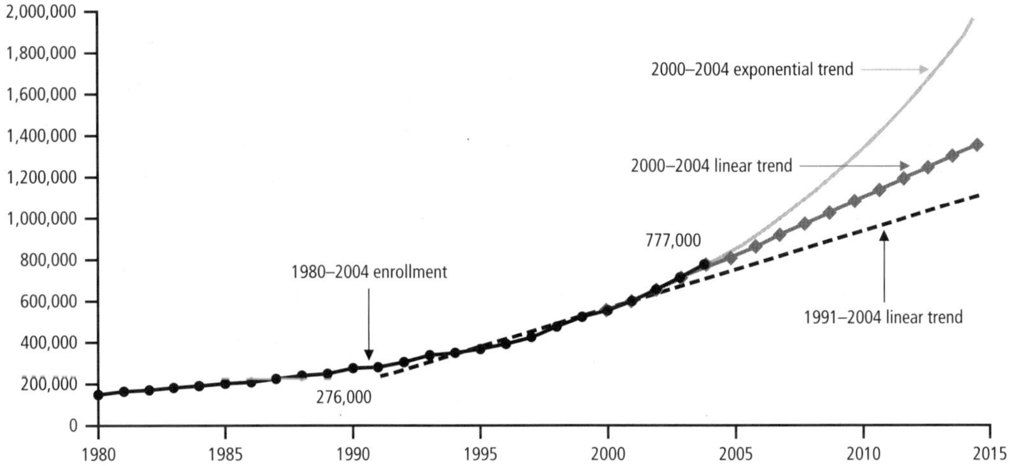

Sources: Data from the UIS, World Bank, appendix table B2, and authors' simulations.

rent number. The coverage rate of higher education would increase from 343 to almost 500 students per 100,000 inhabitants.

- The second projection uses the most recent internal trends in higher education, but it does not take into account the most recent trends in primary and secondary enrollment. It appears that trends for these levels (the secondary, in particular) have been on the rise over the recent years and will affect the social demand for higher education in the years to come. To take this impact into account, a *third projection* was performed, assuming an exponential trend for enrollment (with the hypothesis that the annual growth of enrollment rates increases over the period). In this scenario, the number of students enrolled in higher education in Francophone Africa would be close to 2 million in 2015, or 2.5 times higher than in 2004. In 2015, we would have close to 700 students per 100,000 inhabitants in all of the 21 Francophone African countries.

Table II.1 applies the last projection to each country and shows significant cross-country differences in terms of the future social demand for higher education. For 5 of the 21 countries, the exponential projection (that which has the highest probability of accurately forecasting the demand) points to the need to nearly double the number of slots currently available to accommodate students by 2015 (the Central African Republic, Madagascar, Mauritania, Niger, and the Republic of Congo). For eight other countries, the same projection method estimates a need in 2015 of two to three times the number of slots currently available. In the

Table II.1: Number of Students Enrolled in 2004 and Projected Social Demand by Country

	2004 or closest available year		2015 social demand (exponential trend)[a]		
	Number of students	Students per 100,000 inhabitants	Number of students	Students per 100 000 inhabitants	As a multiple of the number of students in 2004
Djibouti[b] (only public institutions)	1,134	159	13,000	1,601	**11.8**
Comoros (only public institutions)	1,779	225	12,000	1,194	**7.0**
Mali	33,591	251	145,000	762	**4.9**
Benin	40,698	588	150,000	1,653	**3.7**
Côte d'Ivoire	110,472	698	363,000	1,827	**3.3**
Chad	10,075	114	34,000	277	**3.3**
Burkina Faso	24,975	186	80,000	433	**3.2**
Rwanda	25,233	298	76,000	715	**3.0**
Senegal[a]	52,282	506	147,000	1,121	**2.8**
Cameroon	85,790	526	236,000	1,249	**2.7**
Mauritius	17,781	1,773	45,000	3,358	**2.5**
Gabon[b] (only public institutions)	7,941	305	19,000	1,132	**2.3**
Burundi	15,251	216	35,000	360	**2.3**
Guinea	22,223	258	52,000	459	**2.3**
Togo (only public institutions)	24,774	483	53,000	833	**2.1**
Democratic Republic of Congo	170,000	332	363,000	489	**2.1**
Mauritania	11,045	312	21,000	537	**1.9**
Madagascar[a]	42,143	235	82,000	342	**1.9**
Central African Republic[a]	6,352	171	11,000	236	**1.7**
Niger	8,774	71	14,000	74	**1.5**
Congo[b]	11,710	307	18,000	346	**1.5**
21 countries average	724,023[c]	343	1,969,000	694	**2.5**

Sources: Appendix table B2; and authors' calculations.
Note:
a. For Senegal, Madagascar, and the Central African Republic, the linear projection was preferred to the "exponential" projection because it better corresponds to the trend observed over the last few years.
b. Given the low number of historical observations (but especially the high variability of the enrollment levels observed), the projections were performed based on previously corrected enrollment levels.
c. This figure differs from the one reported in figure II.1. In effect, when necessary, the base data were adjusted (for example, for certain countries, the enrollment levels observed are from the year 2000) before performing the projection.

eight remaining countries (Benin, Burkina Faso, Chad, Comoros, Côte d'Ivoire, Djibouti, Mali, and Rwanda), the social demand for higher education should end up particularly high if current trends continue: the number of students in 2015 would be more than three times higher than is currently the case.

These trend projections provide an initial idea of what the social demand for higher education will be in 2015. These projections, however, do not provide a sufficient perspective to set objectives for this subsector. On the one hand, they do not take the constraints (financial and logistical) hindering the system into consideration, and on the other hand, they were made in the context of status quo policies (that is, they do not integrate the impacts of new policies implemented to reform the higher education systems). For instance, no assumption was made concerning the structure of training programs, the role of the private sector, or pupil/student flow management upstream and within the system.

Consequently, it is important to note the following: (i) whether these growth trends will be financially sustainable with the current policies regarding (public and private) resource mobilization and service supply methods, and (ii) if they are not sustainable, what options will be available to the various countries for setting and reaching objectives that are socially and financially realistic.

I.2. CURRENT RATES OF DEVELOPMENT WILL NOT BE FINANCIALLY SUSTAINABLE IN MOST FRANCOPHONE AFRICAN COUNTRIES

These simulations[53] suggest that if no new policies for structuring and providing higher education services in Francophone Africa are adopted, the **current enrollment growth rate will not be financially sustainable.** As a matter of fact, if the growth of enrollment continues in the 18 countries of Francophone Africa for which data are available, and if enrollment is to meet the social demand, public current expenditure on higher education should reach 1.25 percent of GDP in 2015. In 2004, these expenditures were only 0.53 percent of the GDP. To reach anticipated levels, expenditure would multiply by 2.4 in the next 10 years. Given the current policy decisions regarding the allocation of state resources to education (intersectoral budget allocations) and among the different levels of education (intrasectoral budget allocations),[54] the estimated amount of

---

[53] The following simulations seek to verify, for a given objective of higher education coverage, whether the ways of structuring (the desired level of unit expenditure, for example) and financing (the level of the state's budgetary effort and the number of slots available in public institutions) the system result in a balanced budget. If there is a budget surplus, it means that there is room for improving the quality. These basic principles are discussed in detail in box 6. Detailed information regarding the methodological approach to planning a midterm strategy for higher learning can be found in appendix A.

[54] The only simulated increases in resources come from raising the rate of public levy. Similar to the hypotheses used for calculating the cost of universal primary completion by Bruns, Mingat, and Rakotomalala (2003), the rate of public levy in 2015 will represent 14 percent of the GDP in 2015 if it remains below this target in 2004. It will remain at its current level until 2015 if it was initially higher than 14 percent.

resources needed in 2015 will be much higher than that which can feasibly be mobilized (0.64 percent of the GDP). According to this hypothesis, the financing gap caused by current expenditure on public higher education would be $3.3 billion in 2004 for these 18 countries for the period from 2005–15 (see table II.2).

If the current policies are not changed (status quo), then only 3 out of the 18 countries could be able to meet the social demand for higher education: the Democratic Republic of Congo, Mauritania, and Niger. In Niger, the selection process for entering university makes it possible to stabilize enrollment and regulate the system's development (see table II.1). However, this scope (whose value is only indicative) does not ensure that it will be possible to diversify the higher education services offered (technological study courses are often more costly than the general training programs) nor that it can improve the quality of teaching (the structure of public unit costs, which is too favorable to social expenditure, was not necessarily modified in these simulations). As for Mauritania and the Democratic Republic of Congo, the unit cost is relatively low (see table I.5). This weakness is not necessarily negative if it is accompanied by a vigorous policy for sharing costs with students and the private sector in the broad sense of the term.

II. ALTERNATIVES TO THE STATUS QUO

II.1. FROM BUDGET REALLOCATIONS TO STUDENT FLOW REGULATION

The indicative framework of the Fast Track Initiative (FTI) proposes benchmarks to accelerate progress on UPC goals. This financing framework calls for a minimum of 20 percent of public resources to be allocated to current expenditure on education. It also envisages securing 50 percent of these expenditures for primary schooling, leaving 50 percent for all other education levels. Assuming that allocations for preschool and secondary (general and technical/professional) education at the least should be maintained, the maximum allocation for higher education was assumed to be 20 percent of current expenditure on education.[55] This value was used in the alternate scenarios to the status quo despite variance across countries (for example, in Senegal, where the share of overall budget allocated to higher education is currently much higher than 20 percent).

---

[55] This is clearly a best-case scenario, because many countries in Francophone Africa are still far from achieving universal primary completion.

Table II.2: Trend Scenario under Status Quo Policies for Higher Education in Francophone Africa: Public Financing Gaps Generated in 18 Countries[a]

Countries	2004 or closest — Current expenditure as percent of GDP	Students per 100,000 inhabitants	2015 with constant unit costs and share of private sector at current growth pace — Current expenditure as percent of GDP	Resource mobilization: Status quo in policy decisions — Resources for current expenditure as percent of GDP	Accumulated gap 2004-2015 (US$ millions, 2004)	Average annual gap (US$ millions, 2004)	Resource mobilization: FTI scenario[b] — Resources for current expenditure as percent of GDP	Gap 2004-2015 (US$ millions, 2004) — Cumulated	Annual average
Côte d'Ivoire	0.69	1,827	1.72	0.71	809	73.6	0.88	668	60.7
Cameroon	0.41	1,249	0.96	0.41	485	44.1	0.77	168	15.3
Senegal	1.11	1,121	2.18	1.14	442	40.2	0.82	577	52.4
Burkina Faso	0.46	433	2.15	0.58	437	39.7	0.61	428	38.9
Rwanda	0.84	715	3.07	0.98	390	35.4	0.56	469	41.5
Mali	0.41	762	1.29	0.41	259	23.5	0.66	186	16.9
Benin	0.79	1,653	2.01	0.85	247	22.5	0.77	264	24.0
Guinea	0.51	459	0.94	0.64	96	8.7	0.56	120	10.9
Burundi	0.86	360	1.81	0.86	57	5.2	0.77	63	5.7
Togo (only public)	0.61	833	0.93	0.61	38	3.5	0.66	32	2.9
Comoros (only public)	0.29	1,194	1.55	0.29	31	2.8	0.76	19	1.7
Chad	0.32	277	0.85	0.80	8	0.8	0.70	25	2.3
Republic of Congo	0.53	346	0.58	0.53	16	1.5	1.28	(213) No gap	
Madagascar	0.43	342	0.60	0.54	19	1.7	0.64	(15) No gap	
Central African Republic	0.27	236	0.35	0.31	3	0.3	0.56	(15) No gap	
Mauritania	0.36	537	0.59	0.81	(21) No gap		1.50	(86) No gap	
Niger	0.33	74	0.32	0.45	(25) No gap		0.67	(67) No gap	
Democratic Rep. of Congo	0.12	489	0.23	0.33	(38) No gap		0.56	(126) No gap	
All 18 countries	0.53	675	1.25	0.64	3,336	303.3	0.76	3,020	274.5

Sources: Appendix table B1, table II.1, and authors' calculations.
Note:
a. The term "gap" designates the financial deficit. The figures between parentheses denote the financing surplus accumulated over the period 2004-15, indicating the potential margin for improving quality.
b. The Fast Track Initiative (FTI) refers to the *indicative framework* of the Fast Track with the additional assumption that the share of public expenditure on education allocated to higher education is set at 20 percent in 2015. This is an ambitious target in many of the countries analyzed here, given the fact that universal primary enrollment is lagging (one of the Millennium Development Goals), see figure I.6.

BOX 6: BRIEF OVERVIEW OF THE BASIC SIMULATION PRINCIPLES

Each year, higher education systems must face budgetary constraints: the public expenditure allocated corresponds to the amount of resources that were mobilized for this subsector. Three broad factors are used to determine resources for higher education: the rate of public levy (government resources as a proportion of national wealth), the share of public expenditure allocated to education, and the share of public expenditure on education that goes toward higher education. The product of these three factors provides a composite indicator that gives the *mobilization of domestic resources for higher education* in the form of public expenditure on higher education as a percentage of the GDP.

$$\text{Pub. exp. high. edu.}/\text{GDP} = (\text{Govt. res.}/\text{GDP})$$
$$\times (\text{Exp. edu.}/\text{Govt. res.})$$
$$\times (\text{Pub. exp. high. ed.}/\text{Exp. edu.}) \quad (1)$$

Expression where:

Pub. exp. high. edu. = Public current expenditure on higher education
Govt. res. = Government resources
Exp. edu. = Current expenditure on education

Here, as in the first part of this study, only current expenditures are taken into account.

The *expenditures* can also be broken down in a budgetary equation that shows expenditure per student (unit expenditure or unit cost). In the simulations, we assumed that private institutions of higher education were autofinanced, meaning that they receive minimal public subsidies. This assumption holds true in most countries in Francophone Africa, with only a few exceptions such as Côte d'Ivoire.

Using the above expressions, we can hence write the following equation:

$$\text{Pub. exp. high. edu.}/\text{GDP} = \text{Tnbst} \times \text{UC}/\text{GDP} = \text{Tnbst}/\text{Pop}$$
$$\times \text{UCGDPH}$$
$$\text{Pub. exp. high. edu.}/\text{GDP} = (1 - \% \text{ Private}) \times \text{Tnbst}/\text{Pop}$$
$$\times \text{UCGDPH}$$
$$= (1 - \% \text{ Private}) \times \text{Rate} \times \text{UCGDPH} \quad (2)$$

(continues on the following page)

BOX 6: (CONTINUED)

Where:

% Private = Proportion of students enrolled in private institutions
Tnbst = Total number of students
Pop = Country's total population
UCGDPH = Current public unit cost (public expenditure per student) as a percentage of the GDP per head)
Rate = Coverage for higher education (Tnbst)/Pop)

It is possible to break down the unit cost according to its various components, as was done in box 2.

Source: Authors' calculations.

Public resource reallocation in line with FTI benchmarks could transform a financing gap into a surplus in three of the countries under study: the Central African Republic, Madagascar, and the Republic of Congo (see table II.2). If unit expenditure were reduced, only two other countries (Guinea and Chad) could see their deficit shift into a surplus. Most of the countries under study, however, would experience a financial deficit.

Under a student flow regulation assumption,[56] table II.4 shows that **the average annual financial deficit for the 18 countries for which data are available could be decreased from US$275 million to US$40 million** thanks to strict enrollment control. This control would make it possible to reduce the financing gap by a factor of 6.8, a considerable drop. Student flow regulation would also allow six countries[57] (Benin,

[56] Assuming student flow regulation, the number of government-subsidized students in a given country was determined based on domestic needs, as reflected by the country's level of economic development and the structure of its labor market. Results of these estimates are presented in appendix table B6 and in the model simulations by country in appendix table B7. To take account of globalization, which leads some higher education graduates to expatriate for employment, the number of students obtained strictly on the basis of national needs was increased by 10 percent. This rate is higher than African university students' estimated mobility rate of 6 percent (UIS 2006b), and most likely an approximate, best-case scenario (suggesting that higher education in African countries should primarily reflect national economic needs). Applying this method derives a figure of about 1.10 million students (subsidized) by 2015, corresponding to 60 percent of the social demand (1.97 million) estimated previously. Using another method based on the correlation between economic needs (as per the employment growth rate in the modern sector and average replacement rate of labor force leavers) and higher education graduates, one arrives at roughly the same conclusion: by 2015, social demand would be about double the needs of the modern labor market.

[57] In the six countries identified in the trend scenario (the Central African Republic, Congo, the Democratic Republic of Congo, Madagascar, Mauritania, and Niger), optimal mobiliza-

Cameroon, Comoros, Côte d'Ivoire, Mali, and Togo) to finance higher education services reasonably in line with the needs of their respective economies, although some would require maneuvering room in terms of quality requirements (see figures in parentheses in table II.3). Such results assume strict regulation of student flow, corresponding to 38 percent of social demand (versus an average of 52 percent in all countries under study).

The model shows that, despite strict student flow regulation, six countries (Burkina Faso, Burundi, Chad, Guinea, Rwanda, and Senegal) will continue to experience a financing gap. Other strategic tools should thus be considered in these countries to achieve financially sustainable expansion of their higher education systems.

II.2. OTHER POLICY TOOLS

II.2.1. From resource diversification (public/private financing)...

The financing gap highlighted in the preceding scenario was obtained based on the assumption that private sector support of higher education enrollment remains constant between 2004 and 2015. This section explains how, at the same level of coverage (number of students per 100,000 inhabitants), increased privatization of education tends to transfer the financial burden from the state to the private sector. The countries under study are those that would face financing gaps in the preceding scenario despite pupil or student flow regulation (Burkina Faso, Burundi, Chad, Guinea, Rwanda, and Senegal). Table II.4 lists the results obtained.

Two scenarios were considered. In the first, private sector support of higher education is raised to 20 percent by 2015 if initially lower than this target. This percentage corresponds to the current average in low-income Francophone countries. This measure has proven remarkably successful in Guinea (where the financing gap was reduced by a factor of four) and moderately successful in Burkina Faso. In the other countries where the private sector share is relatively high, compared with the African average, the private sector share is left unchanged and therefore has no effect on the financing gap.

The second scenario assumes a record level of private sector involvement that would fully cover the public financing gap. Such a hypothesis would require private sector support of higher education to almost dou-

---

tion of resources in line with the FTI indicative framework's target parameters is also assumed, along with a higher public resource allocation to education of 20 percent (best-case scenario).

Table II.3: Financial Impact of Student Flow Regulation under Status Quo Higher Education Operating Models, 2004–15[a]

	2004 or earlier	Number of students		2015, flow regulations			
	Current public expenditures for higher education (in percent of GDP)	As multiple of 2004 student enrollment	In percent of social demand by 2015	Assuming constant unit cost and level of private sector support	Resource mobilization: FTI scenario		
				Current expenditures (in percent of 2015 GDP)	Resource allocation for current expenditures (in percent of GDP)	2004–15 gap (US$ millions, 2004)	
						Cumulative	Annual average
Burkina Faso	0.46	1.8	57	1.23	0.61	171	15.5
Rwanda	0.84	1.1	36	1.28	0.56	135	12.2
Senegal	1.11	1.3	45	0.98	0.82	69	6.2
Guinea	0.51	1.6	68	0.64	0.56	27	2.4
Burundi	0.86	1.4	61	1.10	0.77	20	1.8
Chad	0.32	3.2	96	0.82	0.70	20	1.8
Benin	*0.79*	*1.3*	*36*	*0.72*	*0.77*	*(11) No gap*	
Côte d'Ivoire	*0.69*	*1.3*	*38*	*0.66*	*0.88*	*(182) No gap*	
Cameroon	*0.41*	*1.2*	*42*	*0.40*	*0.77*	*(318) No gap*	
Comoros (public only)	*0.29*	*1.9*	*28*	*0.43*	*0.76*	*(8) No gap*	
Mali	*0.41*	*1.5*	*35*	*0.45*	*0.66*	*(60) No gap*	
Togo (public only)	*0.61*	*1.2*	*58*	*0.54*	*0.66*	*(14) No gap*	
Republic of Congo	0.53	1.5	100	0.58	1.28	(213) No gap	
Madagascar	0.43	1.6	84	0.50	0.64	(47) No gap	
Mauritania	0.36	1.5	79	0.46	1.50	(98) No gap	
Niger	0.33	1.5	100	0.32	0.67	(67) No gap	
Central African Republic	0.27	1.7	100	0.35	0.56	(15) No gap	
Democratic Republic of Congo	0.12	1.4	68	0.15	0.55	(153) No gap	
All 18 countries	**0.53**	**1.4**	**52**	**0.65**	**0.76**	**441**	**40.1**

Sources: Appendix tables B1 and B7; authors' calculations.

Note:

a. Countries in italics experience a financing gap in the absence of student flow regulation.

Table II.4. Simulation of the Financial Impact of Student Flow Regulation Combined with Policies Promoting Private Sector Support, Assuming Public Expenditure per Student Remains Constant

	2004 or earlier		Resource allocation for current expenditures (as percent of GDP) FTI scenario	2015							
				Scenario 1					Scenario 2		
						Gap (US$ millions, 2004)					
Country	Percent private	Current expenditures (as percent of 2004 GDP)		Percent private	Current expenditures (as percent of 2015 GDP)	Cumulative 2004–15	Annual average	Percent private	Current expenditures (as percent of 2015 GDP)	Cumulative gap 2004–15 (US$ millions, 2004)
Rwanda	42.7	0.84	0.56	42.7	1.28	135	12.2	75	0.55	(0) No gap
Senegal	21.0	1.11	0.82	21.0	0.98	69	6.2	34	0.82	(0) No gap
Chad	20.3	0.32	0.70	20.3	0.82	20	1.9	33	0.69	(1) No gap
Burundi	30.1	0.86	0.77	30.1	1.10	20	1.8	52	0.76	(1) No gap
Guinea	11.1	0.51	0.56	20	0.58	6	0.6	23	0.56	(0) No gap
Burkina Faso	9.8	0.46	0.61	20	1.09	132	12.0	55	0.61	(0) No gap
Total	23	0.68	0.67	26	0.97	64	5.8	45	0.67	(2) No gap

Source: Authors' calculations
Note: FTI = Fast Track Initiative; GDP = gross domestic product.

ble (from 23 percent to 45 percent) in the six countries under study. Experience shows that such an expansion of the private sector is feasible. In some countries, such as Côte d'Ivoire, the private sector share of higher education jumped from negligible figures to nearly 30 percent of the student population in just 10 years. This expansion, partly stimulated by public subsidies, has increased the higher education system's accommodation capacity at a reduced cost to the government. For example, in the mid-1990s, public subsidies per private school student in Côte d'Ivoire were about half the public sector unit cost.[58]

These scenarios clearly illustrate the role the private sector can play in the development of higher education systems. Doubling the private sector's share by 2015 may be difficult for many countries, however, because of a low level of average per capita income. Moreover, increased privatization of higher education may be unfair because it tends to further restrict access to the system for poor students. Therefore, for many years to come, the state will remain the primary financing source for higher education in Francophone Africa. Delivery of higher public education services should thus be designed to ensure equitable access[59] to the system as well as the quality and relevance of its components.

II.2.2. ...To efficiency gains in higher education services delivery

II.2.2.1. Controlled expansion of higher education thus becomes financially sustainable

The scenarios presented above assume that public expenditure per student will remain at relatively high levels (see first part of this study). The scenario simulated here assumes a progressive adjustment of public expenditure per student toward levels compatible with the economic development anticipated for each country by 2015.[60] As shown in table II.5, **public expenditure per student should drop by almost 40 percent on average between 2004 and 2015.** Actual changes in public expenditure per student vary across countries, however, because the current level of costliness of higher education differs from one country to another. Because of relatively low costliness, public expenditure per student is increasing in Cameroon, the Central African Republic, Comoros, the

---

[58] Based on author's estimates derived from data from Bih, Berthe, Kone, and Okon (2003).
[59] Even with the adoption of strict student flow regulation, enrollment in Francophone African countries' higher education systems will increase by an average of 60 percent by 2015.
[60] A decreasing correlation between national per capita GDP and per student expenditure was assumed. Such correlation was used to simulate the unit costs used in this section. This method is similar to that used to calculate the higher education costliness index (table I.5).

Democratic Republic of Congo, Mauritania, and Togo. For the same reasons, unit expenditure remains constant (in proportion to the per capita GDP) in Madagascar.[61]

Table II.5 lists the simulation results. The data show that gains in efficiency in the delivery of higher public education services (resulting in an overall drop in public expenditure per student) have transformed into a surplus in the financing gap, which resulted from student flow regulation without a drop in unit costs (see table II.3). This scenario occurs in Burkina Faso, Burundi, Chad, Guinea, Rwanda, and Senegal. Table II.5 also shows that **controlled expansion of higher education (with student flow regulation) becomes financially sustainable if unit expenditure is reduced.**

Raising public expenditure per student in Togo (by 50 percent) and in the Democratic Republic of Congo (by multiplying it by a factor of six) leads to a financing gap in these countries. In the Democratic Republic of Congo, this deficit would disappear if the share of higher education enrollment sponsored by the private sector reached 55 percent by 2015 (versus 19 percent in 2004), a target that appears difficult to reach. If unit expenditure is multiplied times two at most (rather than times six), the deficit would disappear even in a context in which the private sector share would remain constant. Thus, there is substantial scope in the Democratic Republic of Congo, as well as in Cameroon, the Central African Republic, Comoros, Madagascar, Mauritania, and Togo to improve higher education delivery and quality by increasing unit expenditures while allocating more resources to research, teacher training, and teacher remuneration.[62]

If the financing surplus is low following an increase in unit expenditure, other financing mechanisms must be pursued.

II.2.2.2. Diversifying sources of financing and cost-sharing

Public education institutions can diversify their financing sources by developing **income-generating activities** and implementing **cost-recovery strategies.** Many examples exist in Anglophone Africa. One of the most

---

[61] Because the scenario anticipates economic growth in the countries under study, keeping relative unit costs constant in Madagascar implies a real increase in actual expenditure per student (a 20 percent increase, in the case of this country).

[62] As noted in the first part of this study, education and scientific expenditures as well as research resources are rather weak in most Francophone African countries. In addition, as indicated in box 3, in certain countries, such as the Democratic Republic of Congo, teachers may not be sufficiently qualified. The low levels of teacher compensation in these countries (as suggested in the figures for the Democratic Republic of Congo in table I.7) relative to international levels lead teachers to devote much of their time to short-term teaching contracts in the private sector, reducing teaching time in public institutions and thus negatively affecting the quality of public education services.

Table II.5: Simulation of the Impact of Student Flow Regulation Combined with More Efficient Delivery of Higher Public Education Services in 18 Countries of Francophone Africa

	2004	2015, at constant level of private sector support					
	Public current expenditures (in percent of GDP)	Unit cost: Efficiency assumption		Current expenditures (in percent of 2015 GDP)	Resource allocation for current expenditures in percent of GDP (FTI scenario)	2004–15 gap (US$ millions, 2004)	
		Percent of per capita GDP	As a multiple of 2004 unit cost			Cumulative	Annual average
Democratic Rep. of Congo	0.12	360	6.32	0.97	0.56	**154**	14
Togo (public only)	0.61	166	1.48	0.80	0.66	**16**	1.5
Mauritania	0.36	143	1.31	0.61	1.5	(84) No gap	
Central African Rep.	0.27	182	1.17	0.41	0.56	(11) No gap	
Cameroon	0.41	96	1.14	0.46	0.77	(267) No gap	
Comoros (public only)	0.29	143	1.1	0.47	0.76	(7) No gap	
Madagascar	0.43	189	1	0.5	0.64	(47) No gap	
Mali	0.41	184	0.95	0.43	0.66	(66) No gap	
Benin	0.79	137	0.92	0.66	0.77	(23) No gap	
Côte d'Ivoire	0.69	104	0.76	0.5	0.88	(308) No gap	
Guinea	0.51	129	0.56	0.36	0.56	(63) No gap	
Chad	0.32	199	0.52	0.42	0.7	(45) No gap	
Senegal	1.11	119	0.48	0.48	0.82	(147) No gap	
Burundi	0.86	321	0.45	0.49	0.77	(16) No gap	
Niger	0.33	236	0.42	0.13	0.67	(102) No gap	
Burkina Faso	0.46	187	0.34	0.42	0.61	(55) No gap	
Congo	0.65	84	0.31	0.27	1.28	(309) No gap	
Rwanda	0.84	170	0.23	0.29	0.56	(50) No gap	
Total for all 18 countries	**0.53**	**175**	**0.63**	**0.48**	**0.76**	**170**	**14**

Sources: Appendix tables B1 and B7; author's calculations.
Note: FTI = Fast Track Initiative; GDP = gross domestic product.

famous is the case of the University of Makerere in Uganda,[63] where the percentage of students who paid tuition fees jumped from 0 percent in 1993 to 70 percent in 1999. The introduction of tuition fees did not slow down the growth in enrollment, however.[64] In 1999, nearly one-third of the university's resources came from various income-generating activities (Short 1999).

Such practices have begun to spread in many Francophone countries. In Madagascar, by the end of the 1990s, school tuition fees[65] represented a considerable proportion of public unit expenditure (as much as 12 percent in certain faculties or schools). In Rwanda, in 2002, the Kigali Institute of Science and Technology (KIST, a public institution) generated 35 percent of its budget through various income-generating activities (tuition fees, consulting services, distance learning, on-the-job training, and so on).[66] In the Democratic Republic of Congo, students contributed to more than 90 percent of the University of Kinshasa's earnings at the beginning of the decade—one reason for the low public expenditure per student in the country. This type of direct funding is sometimes viewed as excessive and conducive to inequality, however, because it decreases low-income students' already limited access to higher education. Finally, in Togo, the government recently raised fees for registration and for various student assistance services at the University of Lomé. According to university leaders, this measure resulted in a significant increase in university resources (although the university remains dependent on government grants).

The experiences of these countries highlight the **many advantages of supplementing public financing with private financing,** including an increase in equity. Inversely a higher education system almost exclusively financed by the public sector is inequitable in that it results in taxes being paid by the poor for education services to which very few will have access. A mixture of private-public financing for higher education can increase efficiency, as private financing encourages individuals to choose—and private education institutions to offer—study programs that are more relevant to the needs of the labor market (thus strengthening the correlation between education and economic development, which remains weak in Francophone Africa). In this respect, certain cost-sharing formulas[67] are

---

[63] The case of the University of Dar Es Salam in Tanzania is often cited as an example (see World Bank 2002, 73).

[64] Student enrollment rose from 7,000 to 18,500 between these two dates.

[65] In general, school registration fees are the most direct and largest contribution to costs (with a strong tax effect). See Johnstone (2003).

[66] See Butare (2003).

[67] For more details, see Johnstone (2003), as well as Johnstone, Arora, and Experton (1998).

seen as both equitable and socially acceptable,[68] including student loan formulas that require beneficiaries to reimburse the government once they become gainfully employed. Student loan programs subsidized by governments exist in many countries of the world, including Sub-Saharan Africa.

The success and sustainability of these programs depends on their capacity to (i) promote universal accessibility by placing the necessary funds at students' disposal, and (ii) create a system in which the use of cost-recovery agencies allows for the transfer of some of the financial aid administrative costs to the students themselves. In this respect, South Africa represents a success story (Johnstone 2003).

Political will is essential to implement reforms authorizing higher education establishments to diversify their resources. A study by Ndoye (2004) found that higher education establishments that manage to cover at least 10 percent of their expenditures are almost equally distributed worldwide (13 percent in low-income countries, 17 percent in intermediate-income countries, and 15 percent in high-income countries). Therefore, successful integration of tuition fees in higher education systems does not appear to be dependent on economic factors, but rather on political will. Increased autonomy in the management of resources generated by the higher education establishments could be a particularly effective incentive for implementing such reforms.

The success of financial diversification will ultimately depend on "decision makers' ability to forge consensus among the various stakeholders of the higher education community, making it easier to deal with challenge and disagreement" (World Bank 2002, 87).

II.2.2.3. Strategic tools that reduce unit costs without harming quality

Many strategic tools are available to policy makers and university administrators to improve the use of resources while reducing unit costs.

Better targeting of social expenditures to contain unit costs, increase pedagogic expenditures, and promote equity. Social spending represents a large portion of the higher education budget in Francophone Africa. Cost reduction therefore mandates compressing these expenditures, as the latter are bound to increase as the systems grow.

In some countries, such as the Democratic Republic of Congo, social expenditures are almost nonexistent[69] today because of strong budget

---

[68] For more information on these issues in Sub-Saharan Africa, see Johnstone (2003).

[69] At the beginning of the 1980s, scholarships represented 30 percent of current expenditures on higher education (with an average amount of about US$1,134 per award). By 1989, however, this proportion had dropped to 8 percent (see the 2005 RESEN for the Democratic Republic of Congo).

compression in social sectors. With the exception of these extreme cases, governments in the countries under study have several options to reduce social expenditures (for example, freezing student subsidies—especially during inflation—or introducing excellence criteria for the allocation of scholarships). Cost-reduction tools should be selected based on their tax incidence as well as their degree of political acceptability (Johnstone 2003). Chad, for example, is considering the introduction of such criteria into its subsector strategy for higher education development.

As demonstrated in Francophone African countries, however, radical changes (for example, the introduction of, or significant increase in, registration fees, and the introduction of fees for housing, food service, and transport) are often politically difficult. Therefore, reducing social expenditure should be tested first, while continuing to maintain a given level of student services. Regarding direct financial aid (scholarships), grants to study abroad could be reduced without instigating widespread social unrest.

Regarding nonfinancial assistance, the Gioan and Racamier study (2005)[70] clearly demonstrates that private sector incentive policies can lead to a dramatic decrease in social expenditures by compressing budgets in such areas as student housing (as in Burkina Faso) or food service and transportation (as in Côte d'Ivoire). The study estimated that a private sector program financing 35 percent of higher education student housing would generate net profits for the Burkina Faso government (in terms of investment and operating costs) equal to US$160 million over 10 years.

In the 12 countries of Francophone Africa where social expenditures (excluding support of studies abroad) represent a large proportion of the higher education budget (more than 20 percent of expenditure per student), what impact would a compression of these costs on average unit expenditure have? Estimates indicate that reducing allocations for social expenditures to 20 percent of all higher current expenditures for education (excluding those for studies abroad) would allow for a reduction in public unit costs of about 70 percent of the total reduction needed to bring these 12 countries closer to the average unit costs of other countries at comparable levels of economic development.[71] These results are illustrated in figure II.2.

---

[70] The Burkina Faso study carried out by Gioan and Racamier in 2005 and cited by Gioan in 2006 focused on student housing. The Côte d'Ivoire study focused on food service and transportation.

[71] In model simulations, the allocation for scholarships for studies abroad was kept constant. Nevertheless, decreasing these types of awards is one obvious way to generate scope for increasing other allocations. Cameroon, for example, plans to reduce the number of students it subsidizes abroad by half.

Figure II.2: Reducing Social Expenditures Would Allow for Considerable Gains in the Efficiency of Higher Public Education Services[a]

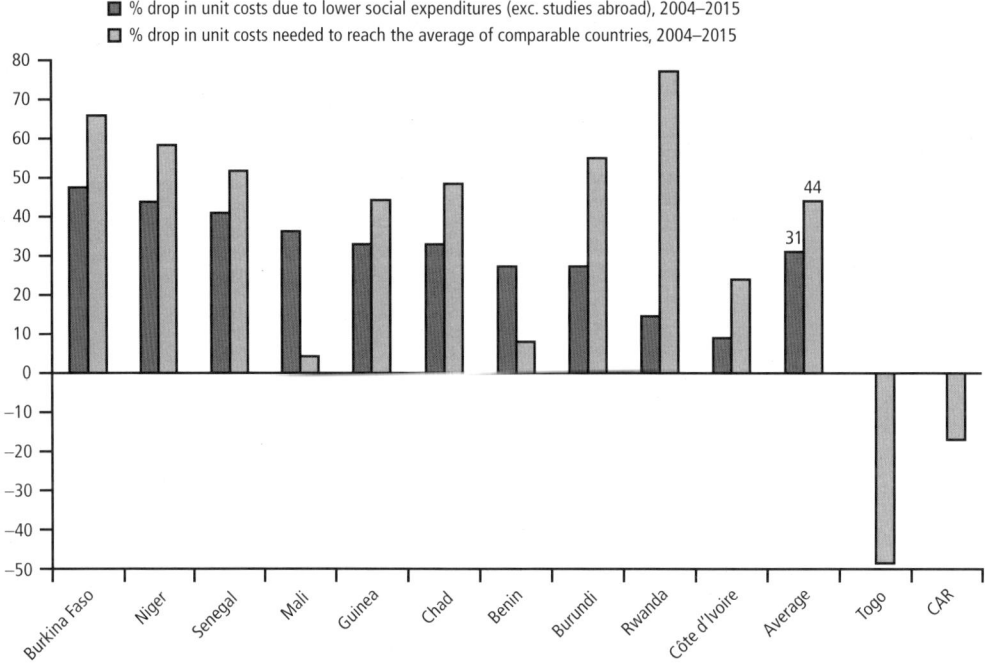

Sources: Sector studies or simulation models; authors' calculations.
Note:
a. In the model simulations, social expenditures (other than subsidies to study abroad) are assumed to represent 20 percent of the unit cost by 2015. For the Central African Republic and Togo, the drop in social expenditures is assumed to result in an increase in other areas of expenditure.

Reducing social expenditures can help regulate student flow and improve education quality. Indeed, in countries where the simulated reduction of social expenditures is significant, the relative share of other expenditures, notably pedagogic, increases. Countries whose current unit cost is relatively low (such as the Central African Republic and Togo) should take advantage of these savings to increase their pedagogic expenditures, funding for the promotion of research, teacher training, and so on and thus to improve the quality of their higher education.

Other strategic tools for reducing public unit costs. Theoretically, *distance learning* offers a variety of potential benefits with a relatively low marginal cost. Despite these benefits, successful implementation may require information technology and heavy investments in staff training and curriculum adaptation (among other resources) beyond the range of low-income Francophone African countries. To be cost-effective, distance learning requires high student demand to support mass implementation of distance learning programs and to keep unit costs below those of traditional programs. Policy measures can be implemented to popularize this type of learning, and in certain cases, education system reforms can be implemented to steer (or force, through student flow regulation) certain students to opt for distance learning rather than traditional academic programs.

Since 1992, Madagascar has offered a distance learning formula along with the introduction of preselection for long university study courses. Its national center for education broadcasting (which has an antenna in Comoros) thus offers alternative training to about 40 percent of higher education entrants who are unable to register in traditional academic programs.[72] Several other countries in Francophone Africa (Benin, Burkina Faso, Cameroon, Côte d'Ivoire, Senegal, and Togo) have (or had, at the end of the 1990s) distance learning units. Available statistics show that only a small proportion of students opts for distance learning.

Improving internal efficiency and reducing the time needed to obtain degrees are important strategic tools to reduce costs. Requiring preselection for entrance to higher education, monitoring reenrollment, and ensuring more selective awarding of scholarships (which encourage students to remain in the system, particularly when they experience difficulty finding employment) are some options for increasing internal efficiency and reducing costs per graduate. In Madagascar, for example, introducing preselection for admission to regular public university programs helped to reduce repeat enrollment from 40 percent in 1990 to 20 percent in 1998.

Numerous other strategic tools can reduce unit costs. The implementation of computerized management information systems (Ndoye 2004) could help increase internal efficiency by eliminating waste caused by processing errors. Computerized systems were found to be effective in the following: financial administration, human resource management (greater transparency in teacher performance and better management of overtime), student records (better monitoring of reregistrations and changes in courses of study), libraries, purchasing, university publications, and admission facilities. At the University of Lomé in Togo, for example, computerized admissions management has allowed for the better use of available slots and teaching materials and facilities.

II.3. TAKING ACCOUNT OF THE COST-EFFECTIVENESS RATIO OF SHORT PROFESSIONAL TRAINING PROGRAMS

Adequate regulation of student flow calls for course offerings that reflect the needs of the labor market. Short professional training programs that

---

[72] This figure is from 1999.

are better aligned with the countries' economies and productive sectors should be envisaged. These programs are usually more costly than traditional programs, and government investment in this area should be guided by cost-effectiveness. High-quality training programs often can be offered at considerably less cost in the private sector. If it is the case, the states should let the private sector support this type of training (as was done in Côte d'Ivoire at the beginning of the 1990s).

Short technical programs in higher education are well developed in Sub-Saharan Africa, where they attract 28 percent of students, compared with 19 percent worldwide (UNESCO 2006b). This type of training is particularly prevalent in Burundi (67 percent of students), Zimbabwe (59 percent), Mauritius (57 percent), Sierra Leone (56 percent), Lesotho (49 percent), Nigeria and Zambia (41 percent each), and Namibia (39 percent). It is less prevalent in Francophone Africa, with participation by 35 percent of students in Rwanda, 32 percent in Comoros, 23 percent in Senegal, 18 percent in Madagascar, 15 percent in the Republic of Congo, and just 5 percent in Mali, Mauritania, and Chad (Mazeran 2006; UNESCO 2006b). This type of technical education may lead to well-paying jobs in national economies that have difficulty absorbing all graduates of regular university programs.

Conclusion

Francophone African countries are facing many challenges in higher education. Boosting quantitative coverage and improving the quality and adequacy of the training offered in keeping with labor market requirements are among the main challenges. Indeed, in these countries, the average enrollment rate is lower than in other countries with comparable levels of economic development (with a ratio of 1 to 2), even though the unemployment rate is particularly high among higher education graduates. Higher education not only acts as a vector of growth and economic competitiveness but also reduces poverty by training and educating populations. This study identifies ways to make education policies for higher education in Francophone African countries more efficient and to develop such education within a framework that is both financially sustainable and socially realistic.

The financial dimension must be considered in any policy for developing higher education in Francophone Africa because these countries, more so than others, are facing major financial, macroeconomic, and sector constraints. Economic growth and public revenues are still low and unstable. In addition, because of the needs created by pushing for UPC, it will be difficult to increase the higher education's share of the education budget (already relatively high) in most countries; this share may even decrease in some of them. Public expenditure per student is high in Francophone Africa: on average, it is 50 percent higher than in other countries with comparable levels of economic development. Social assistance forms a large part of this expenditure, which leaves few resources for academic activities and research. The variability of the cost per student and its composition in the different countries indicate that different policies can be implemented. As a consequence, efficiency gains and a better balance between academic and social expenditures can be achieved.

Because of the high increase in the demand, status quo policies—that is, those that maintain current modes of structuring (the composition and level of public expenditure per student) and financing (the level of privatization in the education sector)—will lead to decreasing the amount of education and financial resources per student and to a deterioration of the teaching environment. The current rates of quantitative expansion, which are estimated to mean a multiplying of the number of students in Francophone African countries by 2.5 between now and 2015, will not be financially sustainable in most of these countries. International experience has shown that countries having undertaken reforms that take these constraints into consideration have managed to develop quality higher education systems.

Tools are available to decision makers. Several tools may be used together to build financially sustainable and socially realistic policies. These policies may regulate and steer the flows of current and future students, implement budgetary allocation mechanisms that tie financial aid to performance, improve governance and encourage efficiency gains in terms of reducing the average length of studies and operating costs (namely by personnel shuffling and sending some with administrative position into teaching positions), encourage the development of private higher education, aim to provide merit- or need-based social assistance, entrust housing and food services to private providers, promote diversifying financing sources, transfer part of the costs to students, and boost the key revenue-generating activities. None of these policies should be given priority over the others. The importance of these tools and the way they are combined must be adapted to the specific situation in each country, and their implementation must reflect the status of social and political dialogue.

For the debate concerning higher education policies to evolve in the right direction, it must based on information that is transparent, abundant, high quality, and available to all actors. This study showed that this is far from being the case in many countries, especially concerning costs, and particularly costs per graduate and the efficiency of higher education in terms of graduates' entry into the labor market. Decision makers must have a midterm outlook that is viable enough for them to defend the choices they make. Financial simulation models must be used more systematically as communication tools to reach consensuses among the system's different actors and partners.

It is possible to continue implementing such difficult strategic decisions if the relationship among the state, higher learning institutions, and all stakeholders involved revolves around greater objectivity and shared responsibilities. Thus, the regulatory framework must give more autonomy to higher education institutions to encourage decision making and initiatives that could lead to better management and must specify the role of the state to direct and more effectively allocate public resources and ensure quality. Clarifying the roles to be played by each actor is a prerequisite for implementing steering and management tools.

This comparative study provides factual information concerning the status of higher education systems in African countries. Its simple goal is to make decision makers more aware of the financial constraints and the potential scope for developing these education systems. To continue making progress toward implementing new policies, this approach must be enhanced by national technical work that places a greater emphasis on the specificities of the different education systems. Awareness of the problems shared by most higher educations systems is being gained in Francophone African countries, and some of these countries have conducted such studies within the framework of a national, global education policy that is balanced and financially sustainable. Beyond analyses and consensuses on the objectives and instruments to be implemented, key decision makers and the academic community in the countries concerned must be involved in the actual implementation of in-depth reforms that inevitably have to be made to ensure the controlled development of quality higher education. Those countries that do propose such reforms to develop their higher education systems in a financially sustainable way will be wholly supported by international development partners.

References

Amelewonou, K., and M. Brossard. 2005. "Développer l'éducation secondaire en Afrique: Enjeux, contraintes et marges de manœuvre." Pôle de Dakar. Report prepared for the Regional Workshop on Secondary Education in Africa, November 21–24, 2005, Addis-Ababa, Ethiopia.

AfDB-Senegal (African Development Bank Group, Republic of Senegal). 2006. "Aide-mémoire de la mission d'évaluation du projet d'appui à l'enseignement supérieur dans les pays de l'Union Economique et Monétaire Ouest Africaine." African Development Bank Group, Republic of Senegal.

Berhélemy, J-C., and F. Arestoff. 2002. "Les stratégies d'éducation et le développement en Afrique." Communication presented at the *colloque de l'Institut de France* on "L'éducation, fondement du développement durable en Afrique," November 7, 2002, Fondation Singer-Polignac.

Berhélemy, J-C., and A. Varoudakis. 1995. "Clubs de convergence et croissance: le rôle du développement financier et du capital humain." *Revue économique* 46 (2): 217–35.

Bih, E., Z. Berthe, R-F-X. Kone, and G-M. Okon. 2003. *Analyse de l'incidence du soutien public au secteur privé de l'éducation en Côte D'Ivoire*. ROCARE and World Bank.

Birgit, Brock-Utne. 2003. "Formulating Higher Education Policies in Africa: The Pressure from External Forces and the Neoliberal Agenda." Institute for Educational Research, University of Oslo, Norway.

Bloom, D., D. Caning, and K. Chan. 2005. "Higher Education and Economic Development in Africa." Harvard University.

Bourdon, J. 1999. "Eléments d'analyse de l'efficacité des systèmes éducatifs et de formation: Peut-on définir une lecture comparative sous l'angle qualitatif de la dépense éducative?" Communication IDEP, June 21–22, 1999, Marseille.

Bruns, B., A. Mingat, and M. Rakotomalala. 2003. *Achieving Universal Primary Education by 2015: A Chance for Every Child*. Washington, DC: World Bank.

Butare, A. 2003. "Activités génératrices de revenus dans l'enseignement supérieur: le cas de l'Institut des sciences, de technologies et de gestion de Kigali (KIST)." Study prepared for the Regional Training Conference on Improving Higher Education in Sub-Saharan Africa: What Works! State University of New York at Buffalo.

Court, D. "Financing Higher Education in Africa: Makerere, the Quiet Revolution." Tertiary Education Thematic Group Publication Series No. 22883. World Bank, Washington, DC.

Davoodi, H. R., E. R. Tiongson, and S. Asawanuchit. 2003. "How Useful Are Benefit Incidence Analyses of Public Education and Health Spending?" IMF/WP/03/227. International Monetary Fund, Washington, DC.

De Ferranti, D., E-G. Perry, I. Gill, J-L. Guash, W. F. Maloney, C. Sánchez-Páramo, and N. Schady. 2003. *Closing the Gap in Education and Technology.* Washington, DC: World Bank.

Foko, B-A., A-F. Ndém, and N. Reuge. 2004. "Aspects économiques de l'efficacité externe de l'éducation au Sénégal." Document de travail du Pôle de Dakar.

Gioan, P. A. 2006. "Les leviers pour des politiques d'enseignement supérieur soutenables financièrement dans les pays francophones d'Afrique." Edufrance.

Gioan, P. A. 2005. *Étude relative à l'élaboration des orientations de politique nationale en matière d'enseignement supérieur et de recherche* (Study of the development of national policy guidelines for higher education and research).

Gioan, P. A., and Racamier. 2005. "Etude relative à l'élaboration des orientations de politique nationale en matière d'enseignement supérieur et de recherche."

IBE (International Bureau of Education). 2001. *2001 World Data on Education.* CD-ROM. International Bureau of Education.

Johnstone, D-B. 2003. "Finance et accessibilité dans l'enseignement supérieur: Droits d'inscription et prêts aux étudiants en Afrique au sud du sahara." Study prepared for the Regional Training Conference on Improving Higher Education in Sub-Saharan Africa: What Works! State University of New York at Buffalo.

Johnstone, D-B., A. Arora, and W. Experton. 1998. "The Financing and Management of Higher Education: A Status Report on Worldwide Reforms." State University of New York at Buffalo and the World Bank.

Mazeran, J. 2006. "L'enseignement supérieur professionnel court en Afrique subsaharienne." CIEP, June.

Mingat, A. 2006. "Disparités sociales en éducation en Afrique subsaharienne: Genre, localisation géographique et revenu du ménage." IREDU-CNRS.

Mingat, A. 2004a. "Questions de soutenabilité financière concernant le développement de l'enseignement secondaire dans les pays d'Afrique subsaharienne."

Mingat, A. 2004b. "Note pour la définition d'un cadre stratégique structurel pour le développement de l'enseignement supérieur au Cameroun à l'horizon 2015."

Mingat, A., and B. Suchaut. 2000. *Les systèmes éducatifs africains: une analyse économique comparative.* De Boeck University.

Murphy, P., S. Anzalone, A. Bosch, and J. Moulton. 2002. "Enhancing Learning Opportunities in Africa: Distance Education and Information and Communication Technologies for Learning." Africa Region Human Development Working Papers Series. World Bank, Washington, DC.

Ndoye, M. 2004. "L'enseignement supérieur en Afrique: problématique des réformes."

OECD (Organisation for Economic Co-operation and Development). 2006. *Education at a Glance: OCDE Indicators 2006.* OECD.

OECD-UIS (Organisation for Economic Co-operation and Development–UNESCO Institute for Statistics). 2005. *Education Trends in Perspective. Analysis of the World Education Indicators.* Montréal: OECD and UNESCO Institute for Statistics.

OECD-UIS (Organisation for Economic Co-operation and Development–UNESCO Institute for Statistics). 2002. *Financing Education: Investment and Returns. Analysis of the World Education Indicators.* Montréal: OECD and UNESCO Institute for Statistics.

Pôle de Dakar. 2003. "Eléments d'analyses du secteur éducation en Guinée-Bissau." Working Paper, Pôle de Dakar, Dakar.

Psacharopoulos, G., and H-A. Patrinos. 2002. "Returs to Investment in Education: A Further Update." World Bank Policy Research Working Paper No. 2881, World Bank, Washington, DC.

Rasera, J-B., J-P. Jarousse, and C-R. Noumon. 2003. *Le financement dans les systèmes éducatifs d'Afrique subsaharienne.* Association for the Development of Education in Africa (ADEA-GTFE), World Bank, Washington, DC.

Saint, W. 1999. "Enseignement tertiaire à distance et technologie en Afrique subsaharienne." ADEA Working Group on Higher Education (Association for the Development of Education in Africa), World Bank, Washington, DC.

Saint, W. 1992. "Universities in Africa: Strategies for Stabilization and Revitalization." Technical Paper No. 194, Africa Technical Department Series, World Bank, Washington, DC.

Schmidt, P. 2005. "Dépenses dans l'enseignement tertiaire en Europe en 2002." Populations et conditions sociales No. 18 /205, Eurostat.

TFHES (Task Force on Higher Education and Society). 2000. *Higher Education in Developing Countries: Peril and Promise.* World Bank for the Task Force on Higher Education and Society, Washington, DC.

UIS (UNESCO Institute for Statistics). 2006a. *Teacher and Educational Quality: Monitoring Global Needs for 2015.* Montréal: UNESCO Institute for Statistics.

UIS (UNESCO Institute for Statistics). 2006b. *Global Education Digest: Comparing Education Statistics around the World.* Montréal: UNESCO Institute for Statistics.

UNESCO (United Nations Educational, Scientific, and Cultural Organization). 1999. *Statistical Yearbook.*

UNESCO-Breda (United Nations Educational, Scientific, and Cultural Organization-Breda). 2005. *Education pour tous en Afrique: Repères pour l'action.* UNESCO, Pôle de Dakar.

World Bank. 2005. *World Development Indicators 2005.* Washington, DC: World Bank.

World Bank. 2003. *Lifelong Learning in the Global Knowledge Economy: Challenges for Developing Countries,* Executive summary. Washington, DC: World Bank.

World Bank. 2002. *Constructing Knowledge Societies: New Challenges for Tertiary Education.* Washington, DC: World Bank.

World Bank. 1994. *Higher Education: The Lessons of Experience, Development in Practice.* Washington, DC: World Bank.

RESEN

(*Rapports d'Etat des Systèmes d'Education Nationaux*, Education Country Status Reports)

BENIN	—World Bank. 2000. *Le système éducatif béninois. Performance et espaces d'amélioration pour la politique éducative.* State Report of a National Education System, Working Paper, Africa Region, Human Development Department, Washington, DC.
BURKINA FASO	—World Bank. 2000. *Coûts, financement et fonctionnement du système éducatif du Burkina Faso; contraintes et espaces pour la politique éducative.* State Report of a National Education System, Working Paper, Africa Region, Human Development Department, Washington, DC.
BURUNDI	—World Bank. 2006. State Report of a National Education System, Working Paper, Africa Region, Human Development Department, Washington, DC.

CAMEROON

—World Bank. 2004. Cameroon, State Report of a National Education System Prepared in Collaboration with Pôle de Dakar (UNESCO-France) and the National Cameroon Team, Africa Region, Human Development Department, Washington, DC.

CHAD

—World Bank. 2005. State Report of the National Education System prepared in collaboration with Pôle de Dakar (UNESCO-France) and the National Team of Chad, in its finalization stage. Africa Region, Human Development Department, Washington, DC.

CÔTE d'IVOIRE

—World Bank. 2002. State Report of the National Education System in Côte-d'Ivoire, prepared in collaboration with Pôle de Dakar (UNESCO-France) and the National Team of Côte-d'Ivoire Working Paper. Africa Region, Human Development Department, Washington, DC.

DEMOCRATIC REPUBLIC OF CONGO

—World Bank. 2005. *Le système éducatif de la République démocratique du Congo: Priorités et alternatives.* State Report of a National Education System, Africa Region, Human Development Department, Washington, DC.

ETHIOPIA

—World Bank. 2005. *Education in Ethiopia. Strengthening the Foundation for Sustainable Progress.* A World Bank Country Study, Africa Region, Human Development Department, Washington, DC.

GUINEA

—World Bank. 2004. *Le système éducatif guinéen: diagnostic et perspectives pour la politique éducative dans le contexte de contraintes macroéconomiques fortes et de réduction de la pauvreté.* State Report of the National Education System in Guinea, prepared in collaboration with Pôle de Dakar (UNESCO-France) and the National Guinean Team, Africa Region, Human Development Department, Washington, DC.

MADAGASCAR

—World Bank. 2002. *Education and Training in Madagascar. Toward a Policy Agenda for Economic Growth and Poverty Reduction.* A World Bank Country Study, Africa Region, Human Development Department, Washington, DC.

MALAWI

—World Bank. 2004. *Cost, Financing, and School Effectiveness of Education in Malawi. A Future of Limited Choices and Endless Opportunities.* Africa Region Human Development Working Paper Series, Washington, DC.

MALI

—World Bank. 2006. *Eléments de diagnostic du système éducatif malien: le besoin d'une politique éducative nouvelle pour atteindre les objectifs du millénaire et la réduction de la pauvreté.* State Report of the National Education System in Mali, prepared in collaboration with Pôle de Dakar (UNESCO-France) and the National Team of Mali, Africa Region, Human Development Department, Washington, DC.

MAURITANIE

—World Bank. 2006. State Report of the National Education System. Working Paper, Africa Region, Human Development Department, Washington, DC.

—World Bank. 2001. *Le système éducatif mauritanien: Eléments d'analyse pour instruire des politiques nouvelles.* Working Paper, Africa Region, Human Development Department, Washington, DC.

MOZAMBIQUE —Mozambique. 2000. *Cost and Financing of Education, Opportunities and Obstacles for Expanding and Improving Education in Mozambique*. Africa Region, Human Development, Working Paper Series, Washington, DC.

NIGER —World Bank. 2004. *La dynamique des scolarisations au Niger. Evaluation pour un développement durable*. State Report of the National Education System, Working Paper, Africa Region, Human Development Department, Washington, DC.

—World Bank. 2000. *Contraintes et espaces de liberté pour le développement en quantité et en qualité de l'éducation au Niger*. State Report of the National Education System, Working Paper, Africa Region, Human Development Department, Washington, DC.

RWANDA —World Bank. 2003. *Education in Rwanda. Accelerating the Agenda for Post-Conflict Resolution*. A World Bank Country Study, Africa Region, Human Development Department, Washington, DC.

SIERRA LEONE —World Bank. 2006. *Education in Sierra Leone. Accelerating the Agenda for Post-Conflict Resolution*. A World Bank Country Study, Africa Region, Human Development Department, Washington, DC.

TOGO —World Bank. 2002. *Le système éducatif togolais: éléments d'analyse pour une revitalization*. State Report of the National Education System, Working Paper, Africa Region, Human Development Department, Washington, DC.

STATISTICAL SOURCES

Government of the Central African Republic. *Lois de finances 2005 et 2006; Ordonnances arrêtant le Budget de l'Etat et annuaire statistique de l'éducation de 2002.*

Government of the Republic of Congo. *Données scolaires et financières pour l'exercice 2004, Direction de la planification du Ministère de l'enseignement supérieur.*

Government of Senegal. 2006. *Modèle de simulation financière de l'éducation*. Ministry of Education and Pôle de Dakar,

IBE (International Bureau of Education). 2001. *2001 World Data on Education, CD-ROM*. International Bureau of Education.

UIS (UNESCO Institute for Statistics). "Education and Financial Statistics." Available at www.uis. unesco.org.

World Bank. 2005. *World Development Indicators 2005*. Washington, DC: World Bank.

World Bank. 2004. *World Development Indicators 2004*. Washington, DC: World Bank.

World Bank. 2000. *World Development Indicators 2000*. Washington, DC: World Bank.

World Bank *Edstats*. Available at http://devdata.worldbank.org/edstats/query/default.htm (last accessed on October 2, 2006).

Appendixes

APPENDIX A: METHODOLOGICAL APPROACH TO MEDIUM-TERM HIGHER EDUCATION STRATEGIC PLANNING[73]

Formulating an effective higher education development strategy requires rigorous analysis of the subsector. If the comparative data presented in the first part of this study can help identify constraints and scopes in terms of available policy parameters, analysis should be carried out at the national level. This type of national or sector study[74] should consider the development context of the education sector as a whole (macroeconomic, demographic, job market, and so on) and, to the maximum extent possible, consolidate any recent operational data (school statistics, financial data, management issues, and so on) and system performance data (number of graduates, publications, research programs brought to fruition, and so on).

Once the diagnosis has been established, planning can start. The planning stage entails several mutually reinforcing dimensions (Mingat 2004b), including the following: (i) a global, quantitatively structural dimension to identify broad parameters such as the number of students expected given the planning horizon, their distribution across broad categories (by education streams or other selected organizational criteria), the level of quality expected for the education services provided, and the implied financial resources; (ii) an institutional dimension to define both the program implementation framework, including the links (financial, contractual, mutual accountability, monitoring and evaluation, and so

---

[73] This section is based on experiences in planning medium-term strategy for higher education in specific Francophone African countries (Cameroon, Chad, and Mali).

[74] This is the perspective adopted in RESENs using a methodology that can be adapted to each country based on the available data. RESENs were developed (or are under development) by national teams composed of managerial and technical staff from the Ministries of Education, backed by the World Bank or other partners.

on) between the central level and the various units for which education services are supplied, and the best practice models for these units; and (iii) a practical dimension dealing with the identified action plans and their implementation schedule. This appendix covers only the simulation model approach.

A.1. HOW TO CONSTRUCT A DECISION-MAKING AID SIMULATION MODEL TO DEFINE FINANCIALLY SUSTAINABLE POLICIES

Various feasibility criteria are used to determine a structural strategic framework (see figure A1). The first is expanding access to higher education as broadly and equitably as possible. The second is offering high-quality academic services and research opportunities. The third assumes that the system meets the actual demand, in terms of quantity as well as quality, of both society and the labor market. The fourth is that the structural strategy developed be financially sustainable, taking into account available national resources, external resources that could be mobilized, and public resource allocations among sectors. The quality requirement is difficult to quantify and includes several different aspects, including economic (adaptation of higher education to needs of labor market), social (focus on quality), and financial (high-value returns to tangible elements such as student-teacher ratio, teacher qualifications, availability of resource materials, and development of research activities, the cost of which cannot be discounted).

The four structural elements in figure A1 correspond to desirable objectives for medium-term development of higher education in a given country. Research on the best possible compromise among these objectives is required to formulate a financially sustainable higher education

Figure A1: Key Structural Elements in Formulating a Higher Education Policy

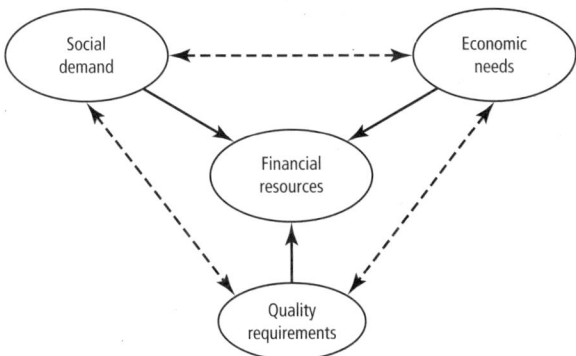

Source: Authors.

policy. The best compromise will be the one that satisfies to the maximum extent the following criteria: (i) social demand, including student flow from secondary education (system "input") plus, in some countries, foreign students (who may represent up to 10 percent of student enrollment);[75] (ii) economic and social development needs, by producing adequately trained graduates and researchers; and (iii) quality requirements, by preserving unit expenditure ratios that guarantee a minimum level of quality while optimizing the use of potentially available financial resources.

The simulation model is therefore based on the following three data: (i) the medium-term (10-year)[76] forecast of potential student flow into the system; (ii) the public financing cap that could be mobilized in the medium term for the higher education subsector;[77] and (iii) the estimated minimum number of system graduates required to meet economic and social development needs. These three data provide the limits within which various scenarios can be simulated. The latter can be based on assumptions about the trend in student flow per the duration of each education stream; unit training costs per education stream; and required investment ratios in terms of student enrollment, average student-teacher ratios, the nature and volume of social expenditures, the emphasis on research, policies that promote private sector involvement, and so on. The best combinations of these parameters will lead to potential scenarios that can be discussed and negotiated.

These scenarios can deal notably with the following: student flow regulation (including a selection process before admission to the higher education system); reconfiguring academic services and research; and revising social assistance policies, the private sector's role in the system, system financing, system piloting and management, and staff policy.

A.2. COMPONENTS OF A DECISION-MAKING AID SIMULATION MODEL

Several types of models can be built to meet the needs of this exercise. These models must be adaptable to the specific characteristics of the various countries and allow for easy use by the principal stakeholders and decision makers. Because source data are often insufficiently precise (hence the need to carry out an in-depth sector inventory), initial esti-

---

[75] For example, 2 to 3 percent of students in Cameroon and Madagascar are foreign; these figures are 4 percent in Senegal, 7 percent in Mali, and 9 percent in Togo (see UIS 2006b).
[76] One 10-year period allows for significant understanding of the impact of the proposed adjustments.
[77] Results of internal decision making at other levels of the national education system.

mates and approximations must be adapted and the model gradually updated as better knowledge of the data is obtained.

To provide maximum clarity, the model can include several interrelated modules. Figure A2 shows a sample format that can be simplified or enriched based on the realities and needs of each country. The various modules are described below.

Module 1: Student enrollment

This module must allow for simulation of the trend in student enrollment over a selected period in the various education streams, based on the estimated number of system entrants and graduates and taking into account the duration of studies. It will include information on the following:

– *Entrants:*
  • enrollment projections for final secondary education classes (system input)
  • estimated *baccalaureate* success rates
  • the percentage of national undergraduates entering the system
  • the number of foreign students entering the system

Figure A2: Sample Structure of a Decision-Making Aid Simulation Model

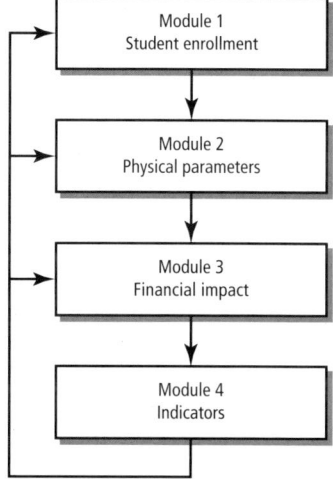

Source: Based on Gioan 2005.
Note: This model was used within the framework of the November 2005 study carried out by P.A. Gioan in Mali: *Étude relative à l'élaboration des orientations de politique nationale en matière d'enseignement supérieur et de recherche* (Study of the development of national policy guidelines for higher education and research). This model was presented during two seminars: one conducted in Mali in January 2006 to train managerial staff in its proper use, and one held in Paris in August 2006 targeting project administrators financed through the French Ministry of Foreign Affairs Priority Solidarity Funds (FSPs).

– *Distribution of students in the system:*
  • regular university programs (science, literature, medicine, and so on)
  • short university programs (2–3 years)
  • engineering programs
  • training of trainers
  • private education programs
  • other types of training, if necessary (distance learning)

– *Graduates:*
  • based on the duration of the study programs simulated for each education stream, the model must allow for calculation of the number of graduates each year for each education stream

The *trend in student enrollment* can be derived for each education stream:

Enrollment year n =
Enrollment year $n-1$ + New entrants – Graduates

– *Estimated job placement rate of graduates:*
  • calculated by dividing the number of graduates by the estimated needs of the labor market. If the latter data are unavailable, assumptions can be made about job placement rates by type of training. For example, the estimated placement rate is 100 percent for graduates of training-of-trainer programs, who generally find employment, and 30 percent for graduates of programs in social sciences, and so on.

Module 2: Physical parameters

This module must allow for the determination of all quantified parameters that affect financial calculations, based on the trend in student enrollment and all formulated assumptions. The quantified development of the various parameters will be carried out over the selected period based on both the enrollment trends calculated in Module 1 and assumed ratio trends. For example, if improving supervision is the goal, one could assume the average student-teacher ratio will evolve over the period from 1:50 to 1:35. This module will cover the following:

– *Personnel:*
  • teaching staff and ratios per student, and the desired trend of these ratios
  • the proportion of overtime and hours of vacation versus standard

hourly requirements for full-time teachers
- administrative and technical manpower and ratios per student, and the desired trend of these ratios

- *Student assistance services:*
  - the number of students receiving financial aid (scholarships, stipends, and so on), and the trend in the proportion of students receiving financial aid (including aid to those studying abroad)
  - the number of government-subsidized student housing units, and its trend
  - the number of government-subsidized student meals, and its trend
  - the number of government-subsidized transportation units, and its trend
  - in the case of incentive-based policies promoting private sector involvement, assumptions about incentive measures can be formulated to estimate the number of students that would be affected (particularly in regard to housing, food service, and transportation)

- *Investments:*
  - the number of education facilities to build, by specifying extensions of existing facilities, new facilities (particularly for program devolution), rehabilitations of facilities, and so on
  - the number of beds to be made available, by specifying investments carried out by government or subsidies granted to private investors

- *Private sector higher education:*
  - any incentives intended for use in promoting this sector must be quantifiable and taken into account (for this purpose, the number of student beneficiaries, if subsidies are linked to the number of students, must be measurable)

- *Research:*
  - for research, the number of programs to be financed could be an indicator

Module 3: Budgetary and financial impact

This module must allow for determination of the trend in higher education system financing requirements over the selected period. It must, toward that end, measure the various cost parameters included in the higher education budget in terms of the following: (i) the various expenditure categories defined in Modules 1 and 2, and their quantitative development; and (ii) unit costs and assumptions about the trend in these costs. The unit costs could be expressed in units of per capita GDP to simultaneously take account of inflation and economic growth. This module will include the following:

- *A breakdown of budget expenditures for reference year* n:
  - investments for each category defined in Module 2
  - staff costs for each category defined in Module 2 (in addition, any specific funds to support the teachers' initial and continuing education may be put in place and evaluated in proportion to pedagogic expenditures for each educational stream)
  - operational costs by type of education stream identified in Module 1 (that is, each education stream could have a different unit cost)
  - research costs based on assumptions about the number of programs to be financed (alternatively, a lump sum allocation could be estimated based on pedagogic expenditures in each education stream)
  - student assistance services for each category defined in Module 2 (the model can be customized to highlight the amount of unit subsidy and number of beneficiary students) (see box 2)
  - measures promoting private higher education
- *Development of these various expenditure categories for each year of the selected period*
- *Development of operational and investment budgets (sum of various quantified categories)*
- *Anticipated revenues, primarily consisting of student registration fees*
- *Public financing requirements to support the required budget*

Module 4: Indicators

This module must allow for verification that public financing needs can be met during the selected period and provide for comparative data from countries at similar levels of development. It must allow for verification that major budget resources are appropriately allocated. The following elements should be included:

- *Macroeconomic indicators:*
  - trend in GDP over the selected period
  - trend in (apparent) rate of tax burden over the selected period
  - trend in the share of tax revenue allocated to the education sector
  - trend in external funding to support the education sector
  - higher education's share of public financing needs (as a percent of the entire education sector)

- higher education's share as a percent of GDP
- *Sector-specific management indicators:*
  - share of the operating budget allocated to social assistance
  - share of the operating budget allocated to personnel expenditures
  - share of the operating budget allocated to academic activities and research
  - share of the total budget allocated to future investments

A.3. USING THE SIMULATION MODEL

This model must provide decision-making guidance by evaluating the relevance and feasibility of different scenarios. The basic scenario must be the trend scenario with which financing needs are simulated based on their projected evolution (without system adjustments). The model will make it possible to test several other scenarios by measuring the impact of various reforms and verifying that they are financially sustainable. The principal elements that could be thus simulated and combined are as follows:

- Student flow regulation
- Share allocated to the private sector
- Allocation for social expenditures
- Relevance and quality of teaching and research services
- Level of self-financing achieved by training and research facilities

The most realistic scenario will be that which both satisfies financing needs and is deemed acceptable by the various actors and partners in the system. The simulation model can be used as a communication tool to develop a consensus. Seeking consensus is crucial because history teaches us that higher education reforms are doomed to failure if they are imposed without broad-based dialog and consultation among the various actors, including the following:

- Technical staff and decision makers at the Ministry of Higher Education (to define a long-term subsector policy strategy)
- The Ministry of Higher Education and other ministries, including those for other education levels, finance, planning, and other technical areas (to decide budget allocations rather than suffer the consequences)
- The Ministry of Higher Education and civil society, such as teacher and student unions, social partners, or other social groups that often have specific interests
- The Ministry of Higher Education and the technical and financial partners (to increase the visibility of the higher education subsector within

the framework of key initiatives that have an impact on the education sector—for example, the Heavily Indebted Poor Countries Initiative [HIPC], sector-based projects and programs, access to competitive funds for innovation and research, and so on)

Although this model allows for comparative analysis of potential reforms, it should not be used as a substitute for the requisite actions or actual reforms that are crucial for transforming these model projections into realities.

APPENDIX B. STATISTICAL TABLES

LIST OF TABLES

Table B1: Public Resources Mobilization and Organizational Arrangements for Higher Education (HE)

Country	Public domestic resources (percent GDP) 2003 or earlier	Current education expenditures, 2003 State-owned resources	Percent GDP	*	HE share in current expenditure on education (percent) 1990	2003	Unit cost of public HE (percent GDP per capita) 1990	2003	Students in private education, 2004 (percent)
Benin	15.9[k]	22.6	3.6	K	24[d]	22.1[k]	351.0	148.9[k]	18.2
Burkina Faso	11.0	21.9	2.4	J	30.2[c]	19.0[g]	650.0	550.0	10.1
Burundi	19.1[k]	16.4	3.1	K	22.3	27.5[k]	1 114.0	718.7[k]	30.1
Cameroon	19.5	15.1	2.9	J	29.5	14.0[j]	165.0	83.5	8.6
Comoros	19.1	19.6	3.7	J	17.3	7.7[j]	138.8	129.9	—
Rep. of Congo	38.8	5.3	2.1	I	32.8[d]	29.8[l]	—	184.0[l/]	8.4[m]
Côte d'Ivoire	17.5	24.5	4.3	H	14.6[c]	16.0[h]	405.0	137.1[i]	31.4[h]
Djibouti	22.3	15.5	3.5	F	12.3	—	498.7	—	—
Gabon	24.4	16.1	3.9	I	—	25.5[h]	—	52.4[i]	—
Guinea	11.1	18.4	2.0		25.1	24.8	572.0	231.0[k]	11.1[m]
Madagascar	11.2	22.8	2.5	K	28.1	17.1[k]	167.9	189.4	7.7
Mali	16.5[k]	16.6	2.7	K	23.2[d]	15.1[i]	—	192.9[k]	12.0
Mauritania	24.2[k]	13.8	3.3	K	22.6	15.7[k]	396.3	108.5[k]	—
Mauritius	18.2	18.3	3.3	J	17.8	17.7[i]	177.1	48.7	17.8[m]
Niger	10.6	24.1	2.5	J	19	13.3[j]	—	564.6	24.6
Central African Rep.	12.0	10.0	1.2	H	24.2	22.2[h]	347.1	156.0[i]	—
Dem. Rep. of Congo	7.7	7.1	0.5	I	35.4[n]	32.8[j]	—	56.7	19.0
Rwanda	12.7	18.9	2.3		15.4	35.0	—	750	42.7
Senegal	18.9[k]	21.7	4.1	K	25.6	27.7[k]	380.0	246.0[k]	21.0
Xhad	10.5[k]	13.1	1.4	K	10.7[b]	23.0[k]	—	385.8[k]	20.3
Togo	16.5[k]	20.6	3.4	K	30.2	17.8[l]	358.0	112.4	—
Francophone Africa	**16.4**	**17.3**	**2.8**		**23**	**21**	**409**	**259**	**18.9**
South Africa	24.6	21.5	5.3	J	21.5	15.5[h]	90.9	53.2	—
Botswana	39.5	4.9	1.9	H	13[b]	18.6[h]	161.5	90.5[i]	100.0
Eritrea	25.5	7.5	1.9	J	—	18.1[j]	—	445.1	—
Ethiopia	19.1	15.9	3.0	I	12.6	17.3[j]	506.6	—	22.7
Gambia, The	18.5	22.0	4.1	J	—	—	—	—	—
Ghana	20.7	25.3	5.2		13.6	—	—	—	4.0[i]
Kenya	23.3	27.6	6.4	J	23.7	—	—	266.1	30.7[h]
Lesotho	39.5	24.3	9.6	H	19.2[c]	18.6[i]	609.1	692.4[i]	—
Liberia	—	—	—		—	—	—	—	—
Malawi	18.6	26.0	4.8	J	24.9	18.0	851.2	—	—
Namibia	32.0	18.5	5.9	J	9.9	8.7[j]	259.5	93.5	100.0[j]
Nigeria	40.2	8.6	3.5	J	—	19.7[j]	—	—	—
Uganda	12.3	30.1	3.7	H	—	15.0[k]	—	—	10.1
Seychelles	36.5	13.0	4.7	J	9.5	17.4[j]	—	—	—
Sierra Leone	12.0[k]	19.4	2.3	K	34.9	22.0[k]		278.3[k]	0.0

Table B1: (*continued*)

Country	Public domestic resources (percent GDP) 2003 or earlier	Current education expenditures, 2003			HE share in current expenditure on education (percent)		Unit cost of public HE (percent GDP per capita)		Students in private education, 2004 (percent)
		State-owned resources	Percent GDP	*	1990	2003	1990	2003	
Swaziland	25.7	13.7	3.5	J	31.9	25.5[j]	305.1	245.9	—
Tanzania	12.1	29.7	3.6	J	17.1	—	—	—	5.4[m]
Zambia	17.9	11.1	2.0	I	22.4[b]	19.4[h]	—	163.8[i]	—
Zimbabwe	23.6	30.1	7.1	E	14.1[b]	—	195.9	201.3[j]	10[m]
Anglophone Africa	**24.3**	**19.4**	**4.4**		**19**	**18**	**372**	**247**	**32.3**
Algeria	40.9	8.7	3.5	J	—	—	—	—	—
Angola	39.0	6.7	2.6	I	3.7	—	231.0	—	32.4[m]
Cape Verde	22.5	21.7	4.9	J	—	18.9[j]	—	284.9	52.6[m]
Egypt, Arab. Rep. of	23.0	5.9	1.3	I	36	38.9[j]	50.4	—	18[m]
Equatorial Guinea	21.2	2.9	0.6	J	—	39.9[i]	—	—	—
Guinea-Bissau	17.8	11.7	2.1	J	—	23.7[i]	—	121.1[j]	—
Libya	—	—	3.5	I	—	20.3[i]	—	13.3[j]	19.5[h]
Morocco	25.8	23.2	6.0	J	16.2	16.3	73.1	110.8	5.1
Mozambique	14.3	21.0	3.0		12.5	21.9	—	791.1	32.1
São Tomé et Principe	24.8	—	—		—	—	—	—	—
Sudan	13.2	16.2	2.1	H	—	—	—	—	—
Tunisia	28.5	20.5	5.8	H	18.8	21.7[h]	115.5	68.0[i]	0.4[m]
Other African countries	**24.8**	**13.8**	**3.2**		**17**	**25**	**118**	**232**	**23.7**
Africa	**21.1**	**17.5**	**3.5**		**21**	**21**	**353**	**251**	**24.6**
Low-income countries excluding Africa	**15.2**	**18.7**	**3.0**		**14**	**17**	**78**	**45**	**26**

Sources: UIS; United Nations (revised version 2004); World Bank; and authors' estimates.
Note: GDP = gross domestic product; — = not available.
* Estimated country group averages (gross enrollment ratio [GER] or students per 100,000 inhabitants) take into account the demographic weight of countries. The GER provides the number of students enrolled in higher education establishments regardless of age, as a percentage of the population of official school age for the first five years of higher education.
a. 1992.
b. 1993.
c. 1999.
d. 2000.
e. 2001.
f. 2002.
g. 2003.
h. 2005.
i. 2006.
j. 1994.

Table B2: Macroeconomic and Demographic Context and Trends in Higher Education Coverage, 1991 and 2004

Country	GDP per capita, 2003 (US$, 2000)	Total population in 1,000s (2003)	1991 Total students	1991 GER	1991 Students per 100,000 inhabitants	2004 Total students	2004 GER	2004 Students per 100,000 inhabitants
Benin	392	6,736	10,873	2.2	226	40,698	4.7	588
Burkina Faso	253	13,002	5,425	0.5	59	24,975	1.6	186
Burundi	100	6,825	3,592	0.6	63	15,251	1.6	· 216
Cameroon	634	16,018	33,177	2.5	276	85,790	4.3	526
Comoros	365	768	223	0.3	40	1,779	1.8	225
Republic of Congo	943	3,724	10,671	3.7	114	11,710	2.7	307
Côte d'Ivoire	597	16,631	28,718	2.2	223	110,472[d]	5.7[d]	698[d]
Djibouti	848	703	53[a]	0.1[a]	10[a]	1,134	1.4	159
Gabon	3,865	1,329	3,000[a]	—	—	7,941[i]	4.9[i]	305[i]
Guinea	431	8,480	5,366	0.8	85	22,223	2.2	258
Madagascar	233	17,404	35,824	2.6	291	42,143	2.1	235
Mali	258	13,007	4,780	0.4	51	33,591	2.1	251
Mauritania	372	2,893	7,527	3.2	362	11,045	2.8	312
Mauritius	4,161	1,221	3,485	2.9	326	17,781[g]	13.4[g]	1,773[g]
Niger	178	11,972	4,510	0.5	57	8,774	0.6	71
Central African Republic	229	3,865	3,840	1.2	127	6,323[d]	1.5[d]	170[d]
Democratic Republic of Congo	87	52,771	80,233	—	—	170,000[f]	2.8[f]	332[f]
Rwanda	260	8,387	3,389[a]	0.5[a]	56[a]	25,233	2.4	298
Senegal	485	10,095	20,300	2.5	269	52,282	4.2	506
Chad	218	8,598	2,842[b]	—	—	10,075	1.0	114
Togo	292	· 4,909	8,969	2.3	254	24,774[i]	4.1[i]	483[i]
Francophone Africa	**723**	**209,902**	**276,797**	**1.6**	**181**	**724,023**	**2.9**	**343**
South Africa	3,026	45,026	439,007	9.5	1,165	717,793[g]	12.7[g]	1,594[g]
Botswana	3,532	1,785	3,900	2.3	280	13,221	5.4	736
Eritrea	163	4,141	—	—	—	4,612	0.9	107
Ethiopia	102	70,678	34,076	0.6	67	172,111	2.1	238
Gambia, The	324	1,426	—	—	—	1,530	1.0	105
Ghana	276	20,922	13,700	0.8	87	69,968	2.5	327
Kenya	341	31,987	33,510	1.2	138	74,402	1.6	229
Lesotho	530	1,802	2,029	1.1	127	6,108[g]	2.4[g]	339[g]
Liberia	123	3,367	—	—	—	44,107[d]	13.0[d]	1,499[d]
Malawi	157	12,105	4,829	0.5	50	5,089	0.4	41
Namibia	1,845	1,987	4,157[a]	2.3[a]	276[a]	11,788[g]	5.3[g]	593[g]
Nigeria	357	124,009	207,982[j]	—	—	1,289,656	8.5	1,015 ·
Uganda	277	25,827	17,578	0.9	98	88,360	2.8	331
Seychelles	6,881	—	—	—	—	—	—	—

Table B2: (*continued*)

Country	GDP per capita, 2003 (US$, 2000)	Total population in 1,000s (2003)	1991 Total students	1991 GER	1991 Students per 100,000 inhabitants	2004 Total students	2004 GER	2004 Students per 100,000 inhabitants
Sierra Leone	141	4,971	4,742	1.1	116	16,625[h]	2.9[h]	322[h]
Swaziland	1,358	1,077	3,198	3.2	368	6,594	4.4	609
Tanzania	309	36,977	7,468[a]	—	—	42,948	0.9	114
Zambia	354	10,812	15,343	1.6	182	24,553[d]	1.9[d]	236[d]
Zimbabwe	479	12,891	49,361	3.9	459	55,689[g]	3.0[g]	432[g]
Anglophone Africa	**1,083**	—	**840,880**	**2.6**	**294**	**2,645,154**	**5.2**	**631**
Algeria	1,916	31,800	285,930	9.5	1,116	716,452	17.1	2,215
Angola	814	13,625	6,534	0.6	68	12,982[g]	0.9[g]	95[g]
Cape Verde	1,290	463	—	—	—	2,215[g]	3.6[g]	478[g]
Egypt, Arab Rep. of	1,622	71,931	628,233	—	—	2,153,865[g]	24.2[g]	2,994[g]
Equatorial Guinea	3,716	494	578	1.5	160	1,003[d]	1.9[d]	220[d]
Guinea-Bissau	135	1,493	—	—	—	473[e]	0.3[e]	34[e]
Libya	—	—	72,899[a]	—	—	375,028[g]	—	—
Morocco	1,278	30,566	255,667	8.5	1,021	335,755[g]	8.8[g]	1,098[g]
Mozambique	255	18,863	4,600[b]	0.3[b]	31[b]	22,256	1.0	116
São Tomé and Principe	334	161	—	—	—	183[f]	0.8[f]	117[f]
Sudan	433	33,610	65,400	2.2	257	204,114[d]	5.6[d]	649[d]
Tunisia	2,214	9,832	68,535	6.9	819	263,414[g]	21.4[g]	2,679[g]
Other African countries	**1,273**	—	**1,388,376**	**5.3**	**620**	**4,087,740**	**14.4**	**1,756**
Africa	**976**	—	**2,506,053**	**2.9**	**328**	**7,455,135**	**7.0**	**842**
Low-income countries excluding Africa	**467**	—	**6,816,548**	**4.9**	**559**	—	**8.2**	**936**

Sources: Various sector studies (RESENs); World Bank, World Bank *Edstats*, World Bank *World Development Indicators* 2002, 2003, 2005; UIS (financial 2002–03 and education 2006 statistics); IBE 2001; UNESCO-Breda 2005; Pôle de Dakar 2002; and authors' estimates.

Note: GER = gross enrollment ratio; GDP = gross domestic product; — = not available.

a. 1990.
b. 1991.
c. 1992.
d. 1993.
e. 1997.
f. 1998.
g. 1999.
h. 2000.
i. 2001.
j. 2002.

Table B3: Share of Investment in Total Education Expenditures and Education Budget Implementation Rate by Category in Some Countries of Francophone Africa, 1998–2004 (most recent year)

| Country (year) | Investment spending (implementation) | | Percent implemented | | |
| | Total | External financing | | | |
	(percent total education spending)	(percent total spending)	Investment expenditure	Current expenditure	Total expenditure
Benin 1998	14	78	72	95	87
Burkina 1999	38	79	—	—	—
Burundi 2004	13	88[a]	—	—	—
Cameroon 2002	11	—	74	93	90
Higher education	*18*	—	—	—	—
Côte d'Ivoire 2000	6	70	24	99	83
Guinea 2000	28	77	—	—	—
Madagascar 2000	29	—	—	—	—
Higher education	*10*	—	—	—	—
Mali 2004	36	90	—	—	—
Mauritania 2003	24	70	24	99	83
Niger 2002	17	83[a]	—	—	—
Dem. Rep. of Congo 2002	10[b]	—	—	—	—
Rwanda 2001	40	—	—	—	—
Senegal	10 (2004)[c]	—	—	91 (2001)	—
Chad 2003	41	82	—	—	—
Togo 2000	11	88	—	—	—
Average	22	81	49	95	86
OECD 2003					
Higher education	10.3				
Other levels	8.3				

Sources: Various sector studies (RESEN); authors' estimates; OECD 2006 (table B6.2). For Senegal, estimates from national data.
Note: OECD = Organisation for Economic Co-operation and Development; — = not available.
a. Does not include the totality of external financing.
b. Limited to the seven provinces controlled by the government.
c. Estimates are based on voted budget lines.

Table B4: Unit Costs of Public Education, in Percent of GDP per Capita, by Education Cycles, 2002 or closest year (low-income countries)[a]

| Regions | Primary | | Secondary | | Higher | | | |
| | | | | | | | As a multiple of | |
	Average	Variation	Average	Variation	Average	Variation	Primary	Secondary
Afriqua, of which	11.7	[3–24]	34.4	[7–66]	300	[57–791]	26	9
Francophone	**11.3**	**[3–20]**	**36.7**	**[14–66]**	**280**	**[57–750]**	**25**	**8**
Anglophone	13.9	[7–24]	32.6	[19–56]	308	[164–692]	22	9
World excluding Africa	11.5	[6–12]	14.9	[7–35]	45	[21–95]	4	3
World	11.7	[3–24]	28.0	[7–66]	233	[21–791]	20	8

Sources: UIS, United Nations (revised version 2004), World Bank, and authors' estimates.
Note:
a. Unit costs in secondary education include general education, as well as vocational and professional education.

Table B5: Student-Teacher Ratio by Education Stream in Three African Countries (public higher education)

	Madagascar 1999	Central African Republic 2002	Rwanda 2001
Grandes écoles (higher education establishments with selective admission)	9	20[a/]	11
Technology institutes	12	25[b/]	Nd
University programs, including	31	31	12
Social sciences, business, and law	82	164	17
Sciences and technology	13	23	7
Humanities and human sciences	28	37	21
Medical schools	44	15	8
Education sciences	n.a.	20	23

Sources: RESEN Madagascar, authors' estimates based on the Rwanda RESEN and official Central African Republic data.
Note: n.a. = no data available.
a. This number includes all higher education establishments.
b. This number concerns only the *Institut Supérieur de Technologie*.

Table B6: Modeling Higher Education Coverage in Developing Countries, 2004

	Estimated models [a]				
	Model 1	Model 2	Model 3	Model 4	Model 5
GDP per capita ($\times 10^{-3}$)	0.484		0.256	0.428	0.324
	(4.8)		(2.13)	(5.9)	(3.52)
Share nonagricultural emplotment ($\times 10^{-2}$)		1.23	0.878		0.414
		(5.5)	(3.21)		(1.88)
1 if Africa (0 if not)				−0.712	−0.63
				(−7.7)	(−6.47)
Constant	2.39	2.17	2.17	2.94	2.77
	(27.7)	(18.7)	(19.25)	(31.1)	(21.8)
R^2	0.27	0.34	0.39	0.63	0.65
Number of countries	64	60	60	64	60
Resideual standard deviation	0.459	0.44	0.427	0.329	0.326

Note:
a. The dependent variable is the number of students per 100,000 inhabitants (common logarithm). The numbers between brackets represent the *t*-statistics.
The simulations of desired student population trends presented in the main text (see table II.3) are based on Model 5. For African countries, including the Francophone countries, the Model 5 equation is as follows:
Log_{10}(*Number of students per 100,000 inhabitants*) = 0.324*10^{-3}*GDP/cap + 0.414*10^{-2}*%*nonagri employment* + 2.14
(In this equation, a value of 60 is assigned to the variable "%nonagri employment" (and not 0.60) in a country where 60 percent of the population is employed outside of the agriculture sector.)
Simulations of the number of students in 2015 have required two additional assumptions:
Assumption 1 concerns changes in GDP per capita between 2004 and 2015. An annual 4 percent growth rate for all countries in Francophone Africa has been used to estimate the 2015 GDP, which divided by the 2015 estimated population (United Nations population projections) provides an estimate of the 2015 GDP per capita. A 4 percent growth rate appears reasonable and is in line with past economic performances of Francophone African countries (see figure I.1). Replacing a 7 percent annual growth rate, a record level, the number of students expected in 2015 remains on average below (in this case, 23 percent below) the number of students that would be expected from the higher education system dynamics (social demand).
Assumption 2 concerns the likely progression of nonagricultural employment between now and 2015. The share of the latter in total employment grew from 21 to 29 percent between 1980 and 2002 in Francophone African countries (from 32 to 40 percent in Africa as a whole, and from 35 to 45 percent in non-African developing countries). Francophone Africa has the highest growth rate (an average 1.6 percent annual increase between 1980 and 2004, compared with 0.9 percent for Africa as a whole and 1.2 percent for non-African developing countries). In these simulations, the authors assume a strong 1.6 percent annual growth rate for nonagricultural employment in the Francophone countries, the share of which in total employment increases from 29 percent in 2002 to 36 percent in 2015.

Table B7: Number of Students in 2004 and Desirable Demand Projections by Country

Country	Year 2004 or closest		Year 2015 desirable demand projections			
	Number of students	Students per 100,000 inhabitants	Number of students	Students per 100,000 inhabitants	As a multiple of the number of students in 2004	Social demand (percent)
Djibouti	1,134	159	5,000	602	4.5	38
Chad	10,075	114	32,000	267	3.2	96
Gabon	7,941	305	19,000	1 132	2.3	100
Comoros	1,779	225	3,000	330	1.9	28
Burkina Faso	24,975	186	46,000	247	1.8	57
Central African Rep.	6,352	171	11,000	236	1.7	100
Madagascar	42,143	235	69,000	289	1.6	84
Guinea	22,223	258	35,000	314	1.6	68
Niger	8,774	71	14,000	74	1.5	100
Republic of Congo	11,710	307	18,000	346	1.5	100
Mauritania	11,045	312	17,000	425	1.5	79
Mali	33,591	251	51,000	267	1.5	35
Dem. Rep. of Congo	170,000	332	246,000	332	1.4	68
Burundi	15,251	216	22,000	219	1.4	61
Benin	40,698	588	53,000	588	1.3	36
Senegal	52,282	506	67,000	506	1.3	45
Côte d'Ivoire	110,472	698	138,000	698	1.3	38
Togo	24,774	483	31,000	483	1.2	58
Cameroon	85,790	526	99,000	526	1.2	42
Rwanda	25,233	298	27,000	298	1.1	36
All 20 countries	706,242	335	1,003,000	355	1.4	52

Sources: Table II.1 and authors' estimates based on appendix table B6.
Note: Desirable projections are obtained under the additional constraint that for each country, the 2015 coverage will be at least equal to the 2004 coverage. In some countries (Benin, Cameroon, Côte d'Ivoire, Democratic Republic of Congo, Rwanda, Senegal, and Togo), simulations without this constraint suggest that the number of higher education graduates already exceeds the 2004 desirable demand. Therefore, coverage is maintained as constant for these countries. In four other countries (the Central African Republic, Gabon, Niger, and the Republic of Congo), simulation results already exceed social demand. In these cases, "social demand" has been retained as an adjustment variable. This appears logical: efficiency in education requires that supply meets demand.

Index

Eco-Audit
Environmental Benefits Statement

The World Bank is committed to preserving endangered forests and natural resources. The Office of the Publisher has chosen to print *Costs and Financing of Higher Education in Francophone Africa* on recycled paper including 30% post-consumer recycled fiber in accordance with the recommended standards for paper usage set by the Green Press Initiative, a nonprofit program supporting publishers in using fiber that is not sourced from endangered forests. For more information, visit www.greenpressinitiative.org.

Saved:

- 3 trees
- 152 lbs. of solid waste
- 1,194 gallons of water
- 287 lbs. of net greenhouse gases
- 2 million BTUs of total energy